WABI SABI LOVE

*The Ancient Art of Finding Perfect Love
in Imperfect Relationships*

ARIELLE FORD

HarperOne
An Imprint of HarperCollinsPublishers

HarperOne

WABI SABI LOVE: *The Ancient Art of Finding Perfect Love in Imperfect Relationships.* Copyright © 2012 by Arielle Ford. All rights reserved. Printed in the United States of America. No part of this book may be used or reproduced in any manner whatsoever without written permission except in the case of brief quotations embodied in critical articles and reviews. For information address HarperCollins Publishers, 10 East 53rd Street, New York, NY 10022.

HarperCollins books may be purchased for educational, business, or sales promotional use. For information please write: Special Markets Department, HarperCollins Publishers, 10 East 53rd Street, New York, NY 10022.

HarperCollins website: http://www.harpercollins.com

HarperCollins®, 📖®, and HarperOne™ are trademarks of HarperCollins Publishers.

FIRST EDITION

Library of Congress Cataloging-in-Publication Data
Ford, Arielle.
Wabi sabi love : the ancient art of finding perfect love in imperfect relationships / Arielle Ford.
p. cm.
ISBN 978-0-06-200375-1
1. Love. 2. Wabi. 3. Sabi. 4. Man-woman relationships. 5. Happiness. I. Title.
BF575.L8F557 2012
306.7—dc23   2011018107
12 13 14 15 16   RRD(H)   10 9 8 7 6 5 4 3 2 1

For Sheila, my bold, beautiful, and brilliant mother, who first showed me how not to "do" marriage, and then the second time around modeled soulmate love at its highest.

WHAT IS WABI SABI?

Wabi Sabi is the ancient Japanese art form that finds beauty and perfection in imperfection. Wabi Sabi honors that which is imperfect, impermanent, and incomplete. It finds beauty in things modest, humble, and unconventional.

Wabi Sabi Love is the art and practice of loving the imperfections in ourselves and in our partners. It is not mere acceptance or denial of the things that may annoy us or even drive us crazy but rather a deep and profound appreciation for the uniqueness of each other.

Imagine standing in front of a four-foot-tall vase with a long jagged crack down the middle. You might be tempted to immediately pass judgment on the vase as ugly or a piece of junk and walk right by. But those who practice Wabi Sabi might place the vase on a pedestal and honor the history and the beauty of its imperfection by shining a spotlight right on the crack.

As with the cracked urn, fissures are a part of ourselves that cannot be changed. Wabi Sabi Love allows us to love and accept the cracks in ourselves and in our partners. It's the hidden beauty that dances right before our eyes, illuminating our uniqueness, calling forth our humanity, and bonding us to each other.

CONTENTS

Contents

FOREWORD

It is with pleasure that I introduce you to a genuinely useful book on a subject of timeless importance: how to create and nurture lasting love. Arielle Ford is a dear friend and has been a trusted colleague of mine for many years. I'm pleased that she has gifted us with this heart-opening and mind-expanding book. My pleasure is multiplied because I know this book will enlighten and change the lives of many people.

As the poet Torquato Tasso said, "Any time not spent on love is wasted." In *Wabi Sabi Love*, Arielle Ford does not waste a moment of your time. She goes directly to the heart of what it takes to make love grow and thrive over time. At the center of this book is a profound insight about how to flow with your experiences in a close relationship. In *Wabi Sabi Love*, you will learn how to embrace and love imperfection: your own and your partner's. Since you're likely to encounter your fair share of imperfection as you proceed along the pathways of love, it helps to get good at dancing with it. This book is a true treasure trove of inspiration and information on how not only to live with imperfection but also to thrive from it.

There are many nuggets to be found in this book, but there is one I'd like to share with you here. As Arielle puts it, "Early on in our relationship we decided that our union would be our number one priority. We promised each other that our choices would be based not on what Arielle wanted, or on what Brian wanted, but on what was ultimately best for our relationship." When I read this passage, I found myself wondering: *Why don't we get wisdom like this taught to us in elementary and high school?* Imagine the mistakes we might avoid and the love we might harvest if we knew a few simple principles like the ones Arielle shares in *Wabi Sabi Love*.

Arielle has a major credential in the area of relationships, and it happens to be the only one that really counts: she has thrived for many years in a wonderful relationship with her husband, Brian Hilliard. Kathlyn and I have been with Arielle and Brian on dozens of occasions, and we can testify that her relationship is a living example of what she teaches.

Relationships of the quality that Arielle and Brian enjoy do not thrive over time by chance or even by good karma. They're the result of the dedicated application of good ideas and good skills. *Wabi Sabi Love* has an abundance of both, and for that reason, as well as many others, I recommend it to you highly.

GAY HENDRICKS, Ph.D., author of *Five Wishes* and
The Big Leap; coauthor (with Kathlyn Hendricks, Ph.D.)
of *Conscious Loving* and *The Conscious Heart*

Introduction

We come to love not by finding a perfect person, but
by learning to see an imperfect person perfectly.
—*Sam Keen*

Love. It's right up there with air, food, and water as one of
the most vital ingredients for existence. Love nourishes our
souls and arouses our deepest desires. And yet, for many
people, it's the hardest thing to find. Even harder still is
sustaining that love once you've found it.

When it comes to making love last, the reality is pretty
unsettling. Right now, 50 percent of first marriages, 67 percent of second marriages, and 74 percent of third marriages end in divorce. But however grim the statistics, there

is hope for keeping love alive. A new paradigm is on the horizon, one that has the power to shift your focus from all that seems wrong to all that is right.

Even if you're blessed to be with someone who is compatible with you on a physical, emotional, or spiritual level, it's highly likely that there is one thing, or perhaps a handful of things, about him or her that you wish were just a little different. Maybe you wish your partner were a more passionate lover or a better listener, didn't leave piles of clothes all over the house, or shared more of your creative interests. If you've ever woken up to that feeling of "if only things were different," you're not alone.

The fact is our culture has conditioned us to expect perfection from ourselves and others, and this expectation often leads us into a perpetual state of frustration and dissatisfaction. The human mind can be a fault-finding machine uniquely equipped to focus with laserlike precision on the few things that are lacking, rather than on the bigger picture of all that we have in abundance. If, like so many, you've lost sight of the forest of your deeper love for your partner through the trees of his or her imperfections, the tools and skills you will learn in this book will allow you to see yourself and your partner in an entirely new light, strengthen the bond that brought you together in the first place, and take your relationship to a whole new level.

This book is firmly rooted in the belief that how you choose to see things informs the way they appear for you. For anyone in a long-term relationship, you know how quickly a little quirk and idiosyncrasy can progress from a rub to a burn. How often do you find yourselves arguing over the same little things? But what if, instead of focusing your attention on trying to change that one thing about your partner, you had the ability to actually change the way you look at that one thing? Suddenly, the focus of everything in your relationship would shift.

How will you get to that seemingly unreachable place? You will learn to apply the timeless principles of Wabi Sabi. Based on the ancient Japanese aesthetic of finding beauty in imperfection, *Wabi Sabi Love* applies this concept to love relationships. It is the art of loving your partner's imperfections rather than indulging in the fantasy that your relationship can fire on all cylinders only when both people are acting perfectly and behaving in ways that are acceptable to the other.

Just imagine the possibilities that would open up in your relationship if you could learn to accept, embrace, and even find the gift in your partner's imperfections. It is not just about tolerating our partners' so-called flaws, but actually finding the perfection in all that is imperfect about them. By learning to live Wabi Sabi Love, you will create a heartfelt, loving, long-lasting, committed, joyful relationship that lights you up as a couple, knowing that you are greater together than apart and that your bond will be forever stronger, deeper, and more meaningful as a result of embracing these practices.

I remember being spellbound when I first came across the concept of Wabi Sabi. It was late afternoon on a cold November day more than twenty years ago. I was gazing out my office window, enjoying the western sky as it turned shades of crimson with splashes of orange light around the setting sun. I picked up a magazine and came across an article with a striking black-and-white photograph of a large Asian urn sitting on a pedestal, with a long, crooked crack down the middle. The crack was highlighted by gallery lighting. Huh? It did not compute. The headline read, "The Art of Wabi Sabi."

Curious, I began reading about this exotic-sounding phrase. In the world of Wabi Sabi, the urn in the photograph was even more beautiful and valued *because* of the crack, because of its imperfection. Singer and poet Leonard Cohen clearly expressed this basic Wabi Sabi principle in his haunting song "Anthem": "Ring the bells that still can ring; forget your perfect offering. There is a crack in everything; that's how the light gets in."

Seeing the ways that Wabi Sabi helps to illuminate the hidden beauty in life had an immediate and profound impact on me, and it wasn't long before I began to realize how this ancient art form relates to love. So many things began to make sense. I mean, I already knew I wasn't perfect and wasn't capable of perfection, but I had never entertained the idea that not only should I *not* strive for perfection, but that my imperfection is in its own way *more valuable than perfection* itself.

I sensed the weight of the world lifting off my shoulders. I could now breathe a little deeper and with more ease. The mess of papers on my desk was no longer evidence of my disorganized mind but rather a testament to my creativity and hard work. The stain on my skirt, obtained at a lunch meeting, was no longer embarrassing proof of my klutzy cutlery skills, but instead proof of my strong appetite for nourishment and for life. I decided then and there to become a Wabi Sabi artisan, and what started as simply a sincere desire to honor the imperfection in myself and others soon became a deliberate way of life.

Once I manifested Brian—my soulmate—I wanted to see if two people could apply the principles of Wabi Sabi toward a long-term, committed relationship, while still preserving the juicy joy and magic that brought them together.

I soon learned that Wabi Sabi holds the key to everlasting love.

The idea of accepting imperfection isn't something I swallowed easily. After all, I come from a long line of gutsy, competent women who know how to "make things happen." My strong-willed grandmother, Ada, used her Irish sweepstakes earnings to move her family from Brooklyn to Miami to set up a new family business back in the day when women "didn't do such things." Following the maternal lineage, my mother, Sheila, is an adventurous, fun-loving, and incredibly beautiful powerhouse. She's confident, smart, and very assertive—a successful businesswoman long before she'd heard of Gloria Steinem. Mom raised me to take care of myself, with little emphasis on the actual feelings of the people around me. Who had time for that? Toughen up and get it done was her motto. The fact is, I would not be the woman I am today had it not been for my mother's powerful role-modeling. And by the same token, I also realized fairly early on in my relationship with Brian that the take-charge attitude that served me so well at work was more than a little counterproductive at home.

One afternoon, as I caught myself with my hand on my hip about to wag a finger at my fiancé, Brian—to vehemently make a point about something—I stopped myself cold. Oh God. I was on the verge of being overbearing, even bitchy. I was so lost in my own needs and wants that I'd totally ignored those of the man I cared about more than anyone—the man I'd been searching for my whole life! This was not the woman I had fantasized about being in my soulmate relationship. Powerless, I felt the stronghold of judgment and intolerance taking over. What could I do?

In a flash of inspiration, I told Brian that if he ever saw me behaving this way again—which I guessed, rather prophetically, would be inevitable—he had my total permission to kindly ask:

"Is Sheila in the room?"

Referencing my mom, Sheila, whom I absolutely adore, would be a playful way of reminding me that while my strong, opinionated communication style keeps things at the office on track, I needed to dial it back a few notches in order to maintain a peaceful home. Brian laughed and readily agreed. Then, being the loving and evolved guy that he is, he immediately reciprocated and threw me a major bone.

"If you ever find me giving you the silent treatment or becoming too paternalistic," he said, *"you have my permission to call me Wayne."*

Oh. This was big. Wayne is Brian's father—a strong and important figure in his life—but I knew his dad didn't communicate his feelings enough and Brian didn't want to model that behavior.

This is how, early on in our relationship, my man and I discovered lighthearted and nurturing ways to diffuse potentially touchy subjects. I hadn't yet connected all the dots to know that we were practicing the ancient art of Wabi Sabi. All I knew at the time was that our interaction felt grown-up and mature, while also being playfully creative and extremely healing. We were both sort of stunned by it, happily amused. It had been so simple—no anger or drama—but at the same time completely life changing. We look back on that moment as a profound turning point in each of our lives: a new way of relating that had somehow eluded us in earlier relationships. And we both believe that had we not gone this route—that of working gently with each other's imperfections—we would have thrust ourselves over the cliff in similar fashion to our previous relationships, ending up emotionally battered, bruised, and—once again—alone.

Thankfully, we were ready. We learned how to apply the art of Wabi Sabi to gift to each other our best selves, flaws included, and we've never turned off the Wabi Sabi spigot. It is without a doubt the secret to our successful soulmate relationship. This ancient practice has brought me . . . us . . . more joy and love than the two of us could ever have dreamed, and it's something I know you, too, can experience!

After the successful release of *The Soulmate Secret*, friends and readers alike asked two questions: Now that I've found love, how do I maintain that love for the rest of my life? And, how do I turn the lover I'm already with into my soulmate? While *The Soulmate Secret* unveiled the principles for *attracting love*, this book now offers ways for *living that love* in a sustainable fashion.

From this book you will benefit from the wisdom that I unearthed along my journey as well as that of many others who have used Wabi Sabi principles to discover a deeper and more fulfilling love. I will share amazing, true-life stories that will give you a vast array of ideas for implementing Wabi Sabi into your everyday life and relationships. You will learn to apply humor, listening, intimacy, and generosity at precisely those moments where you would normally retreat. The fact is that even though it's simple, love, as you know, is rarely easy.

For instance, initially I thought that once I'd found my soulmate, our love would evolve naturally. We'd be living on autopilot, happily floating through one delicious day after another. If only! All couples—even soulmates—have challenges to face and obstacles to overcome in romantic partnership. This book illumines the path to triumphing over our imperfections, not by denying or tolerating them, but by knowing full well what they are and celebrating them!

In these pages you will learn to apply the wisdom of Wabi Sabi to minimize conflict and create a deeper, more loving relationship. Learning to live Wabi Sabi Love in every moment won't happen overnight. However, when you remember the simple tenants of Wabi Sabi—to find the perfection and beauty of imperfection in both yourself and your beloved, you will find that you can let go of issues and challenges much faster, while transforming yourself and your relationship in the process.

With each chapter dedicated to tackling one Wabi Sabi Love practice at a time, the book is designed to help you develop tools and insights to fulfill the promise of your soulmate partnership. It is not about accepting harmful or unhealthy behavior, but about integrating your partner's full beingness, and your own, into a sustainable, everlasting relationship.

Wabi Sabi Love will show you how to cultivate love for yourself and for your partner, especially on the days when one of you is being difficult or stubborn, acting out, spinning off in a million directions, refusing to listen, skipping commitments, spewing negativity, indulging in a pity party, shutting down, closing off, or being generally cranky, moody, and unfit for human consumption. Does this sound familiar?

If you find your toad turned prince/princess has warts after all, welcome to the club. You may not be perfect, but through the practices laid out in this book, your love can be.

Throughout the book, I have chosen to randomly alternate between the "he" and "she" forms because Wabi Sabi Love applies to everyone!

It is my dream that you will use the insights, tools, stories, and practices offered in this book to experience more love, more joy, more compassion, and more peace with yourself and with your beloved. Now, more than ever, the planet needs the high vibration that authentically happy couples radiate—so let's get started!

Wishing you a lifetime of Wabi Sabi Love,

ARIELLE FORD
La Jolla, California

PLEASE NOTE
Practicing Wabi Sabi Love is *not* an invitation to go into denial or accept bad behavior or harmful situations. In the event you find yourself in an abusive relationship, you are advised to seek professional counsel immediately.

ONE

Growing a Generous Heart

Teach this triple truth to all: A generous heart, kind
speech, and a life of service and compassion are the
things which renew humanity.—*Buddha*

As with most new couples, when Brian and I first married,
we experienced several months of true bliss. But as anyone
will tell you, marriage is not the same as the romancing
prior to the wedding. Have you ever noticed we never really
learn what happens to Cinderella after the prince sweeps
her off her feet and they ride off together into the sunset?
What no one tells you is that in real life you have to learn
to live with each other's habits, quirks, and, yes, downright
annoyances.

While we were showered with numerous well wishes from friends and family, the one wedding gift we didn't receive was the handbook on how to have a great partnership. And as you can imagine, being single for forty-four years didn't exactly train me to share my life with anyone. As a businesswoman, I was used to making the decisions and calling the shots about where I was going, what I was doing, when, and with whom.

Brian, on the other hand, was a former successful athlete who had spent his life being a team player, caring deeply about how his actions affected other people and the world around him.

Early on in our relationship we decided that our union would be our number one priority. We promised each other that our choices would be based not on what Arielle wanted, or on what Brian wanted, but on what was ultimately best for our relationship. This shared commitment meant that when we encountered the inevitable disagreements and upsets, no one would threaten to walk out and both of us would take responsibility for finding a solution.

Together we explored couples workshops to learn heart-opening strategies to keep our love on track, and we always kept the lines of communication wide open. We shared our deepest thoughts and dreams as well as our imperfections and fears.

We have been fortunate to find guidance among our circle of friends and colleagues who are happily married, generous souls who have graciously shared their wisdom with us. Many of them—and others who have successfully navigated choppy marital waters—share their stories of turning conflict into connection and compassion in these pages.

Over the past fourteen years, Brian and I have created a life together that far exceeds my wildest imagination. When I've had a full day, I sometimes leave my shoes lying about. And wouldn't you know? Every now and then Brian will find one, get down on one knee, and place the shoe tenderly on my foot, proving that married life does indeed have its fairy-tale moments. And then there are those times when you're both vying for the remote or have two totally different ideas about what a date night should include, and you wonder how two seemingly opposite people could ever find long-term bliss.

If you know anything about the Law of Attraction, you know that you first have to declare your vision before it can become reality. When I was creating my soulmate wish list, I was very careful to list every statement in a positive way, such as, "He will be loving, kind, and generous." Making positive statements about your intentions is an old talk-to-the-Universe trick since the Universe simply cannot hear the word "not." According to the Law of Attraction, if you say, "I do *not* want X, Y, or Z," you will end up getting just that. Although I knew this, there was one must-have requirement that I never did figure out how to position in a positive light, so I simply wrote: "He will *not* be a football fanatic."

Having grown up with a father and a brother who lived, breathed, and talked football 24/7, I often felt as if football was my nemesis in my ongoing competition for my father's attention. The truth is, I hate football, and I just couldn't imagine spending my life with someone who had football blaring on the TV. Truthfully, I'd rather be alone than be subjected to the sound of crashing helmets and the grunts of men in tight pants chasing a pigskinned orb to the beat of seventy thousand cheering fans.

Wouldn't you know? What I resisted persisted. Brian was indeed a huge sports fan—for basketball! Okay, not football exactly, but the similarities were glaring. He comes by it honestly as a former player, but that didn't change the fact that I wasn't sure, at first, that I'd be able to overcome what I perceived to be this most harrowing obstacle. Would I have to compete for his attention, just as I had to for my father's time and focus?

It would be unfair of me to put down the entire world of sports in one fell swoop. After all, those athletes work hard toward their goals, engaging in countless hours of practice while nobody is looking. I mean who doesn't get goose bumps when watching the Olympics? I have shed a tear or two on occasion, watching those medalists stand reverently on the award platform. In truth, it wasn't the actual notion of organized sports that put me off early in my relationship with Brian. It was the idea of competing for my partner's attention and playing second string to a pack of men on a flat-screen TV.

I decided to face the first of many tests by opening myself up to the possibility of actually loving sports. Could it really be all that bad? What might I gain by broadening my thinking? More important, what would I lose if I didn't try to find something positive about my husband's passion? It was time to do some digging, and fortunately I quickly found some research that substantiated my belief that incompatibilities are an inherent part of all relationships.

For the past thirty-five years psychologist and researcher John Gottman, Ph.D., has been studying married couples, and he has found that every happily married couple has somewhere around ten irreconcilable differences. In other words, scientific studies have now proved that having differences in a happy marriage is normal! What a relief!

Not surprisingly, Gottman found that the top two irreconcilable differences are about finances and children. The other biggies include sex, in-laws, housework, political views, communication, balance between home and work, and personal idiosyncrasies. According to Susan Boon, Ph.D., a social psychologist at the University of Calgary, the secret lies in coming to terms with the differences rather than trying to solve the unsolvable. The Wabi Sabi solution is to embrace the tastes, opinions, preferences, and unique viewpoints that make each of us individuals, rather than trying to eliminate them.

These claims all sounded really good in theory. But would I be able to truly overcome my sports phobia and celebrate our diversity with a full-blown embrace?

WABI SABI PRINCIPLE

Having differences is inevitable. What matters is how we manage the differences, and this is where becoming a Wabi Sabi artisan really pays off.

Drawing on the Wabi Sabi lessons learned by my friend Moji, I realized that there was, in fact, a way out of my quandary. Moji, a smart woman whom I greatly respect, came up against a similar challenge when she fell in love with Jason, a football fanatic of the highest order. Her approach opened my eyes to the possibility that there was indeed a Wabi Sabi solution in my future.

FALLING IN LOVE WITH FOOTBALL

It was only their third date when Jason suggested to Moji that the two spend it watching a very "important" football game. Although these words landed for Moji with a thud, she tried to keep an open mind.

"My son had just started playing football as a freshman in high school," she said, "so I was no stranger to the game. I quickly picked up the basics about this rough-and-tumble sport, but spending our date night watching grown men pound one another into submission was not my idea of romance!"

It was the beginning of football season, and Jason and Moji were just getting to know each other. And even though Jason's football was a part of nearly every conversation they had, they still developed a strong bond that moved beyond the sport itself. A definite spark had been ignited.

"Before each game," she recollected, "he would feverishly update me on all the players, stats, and injury reports. During the games, he would explain in detail the complexities and nuances of each play. His true passion for this game was undeniable."

A few weeks into the season, Moji came to a critically important realization about the man she was falling in love with. Her outgoing, athletic, and very funny new love interest seemed to have a fatal flaw: he was literally obsessed with football and everything related to it.

It wasn't long before Moji felt as though she were competing for Jason's attention. She began to wonder, *Is it going to be me or football?* She was faced with a conundrum. Should she tolerate the sport and pretend she was having fun watching it, or should she throw a fit every time there was a game on? It was tempting to give in to one of those options, but realizing that she and Jason had true potential, she decided that she really wanted to enjoy her time with him and not just fake it. And putting up a fight every time he mentioned football seemed like a surefire way to end the relationship.

And then she thought, *Why not me and football?* Moji seriously pondered what it would take to make her relationship with Jason work and, more important, flourish. She thought about the elements of football. It's a bunch of great-looking athletic men tackling one another. It involves speed, precision, and strategy. Her thoughts started reeling as she considered the sport's redeeming qualities.

Finally she came to a conclusion.

"The only thing for me to do is to dive into this with mind, body, and spirit to really learn the game. Then we will see if I love it too."

Moji began asking questions about different positions

and play calls. She even carried a little notepad to take notes as she learned about NFL teams, players, and even head coaches.

"Before I knew it, I was hooked. I am not kidding you! I loved football!"

Serendipitously, during football season the following year, Jason asked Moji to marry him. Their wedding took place shortly after the season ended.

Now, five years later, they plan their social life around all levels of football, whether it's high school, college, or professional games, and they love every minute of it.

"My girlfriends think I do this for my husband, but the truth is, I am doing this for myself. I have become a full-blown football junkie!"

While Moji learned to love football, Jason had to learn to embrace a few things about Moji—the first being her parenting style. A lifetime bachelor, Jason suddenly found himself in the position of stepfather of a teenage son, a role he admits was a great challenge for him. "Being a stepdad doesn't come with a manual. I'm not an enforcer type, but more of a happiness and harmony kind of guy." Having grown up in a household in which he was required to make his own bed and wash his own dishes, he had a hard time accepting Moji's lenient approach to raising her only child. "She says the reason she does everything for him is that she's Persian," he explained. It took a while for Jason to accept her way of doing things, but he soon realized that "A happy wife equals a happy life."

Moji's willingness to explore where her lover's interests might take her and Jason's ability to embrace Moji's parenting style are two clear illustrations of what it means to have a generous heart. We may never fully agree with how our significant others see things, but we can learn to accept, honor, and respect their viewpoints as their own and as valid. Moji and Jason discovered that their traits each had deep cultural roots. Rejecting either aspect would have meant the end of their relationship; by accepting their differences, they deepened their bond.

While Moji's full embrace of football is admirable, finding acceptance for my husband's own sports fanaticism is something that admittedly took me a long time to develop.

WABI SABI PRINCIPLE

Embracing the most fundamental aspects of your partner seals the bond in your relationship.

In the early days of our relationship, I discovered that Brian would occasionally watch a football game (usually a playoff game or the Super Bowl), but he had a near freakish passion for basketball. You could say he comes from a family that is basketball crazed, whether it's high school, college, or the NBA. Believe me when I say these folks *eat, pray, and love* basketball. On my first visit to Oregon to meet Brian's family, he took me to my first professional NBA game to see the Portland Trailblazers play in the Rose Garden. In true Brian Hilliard fashion, we had courtside seats that cost about as much as a midsize vehicle. I was not prepared for the explosion of sound, the bright lights, or the intensity of the crowd. As a highly sensitive person (HSP), I found myself trapped in a nightmarish situation. My nervous system was overwhelmed. By the end of the first half, I was on the verge of a major headache.

Brian was very understanding and assured me it was quite all right with him if we left the game. We went to a quiet romantic café for dinner and spoke about life, love, and our future. The one topic we avoided was basketball.

During the next few years, I heard a little bit about Brian's college-jock days as a basketball player for the Oregon State University Beavers, but Brian is very humble and I really just didn't get the magnitude of his athleticism. Then on one of our later trips to Portland we went to a resort at Mount Hood for a birthday party for one of Brian's closest friends. We were seated next to two adorable young women whose fathers had also attended OSU. At one point in the conversation, one of the women asked Brian what his last name was.

When he replied, "Hilliard," the two women literally screamed in unison.

"Brian Hilliard? You're really Brian Hilliard?"

"Yes," he said, proudly but quietly.

"Oh my God, my dad is going to die when he finds out we met you! You have always been one of his favorite Beavers of all time! He just loved the way you played."

I looked at my husband and thought, *Wow. I've married a jock. Who would have guessed?* I didn't know a thing about basketball, but I was about to learn. During the first six months of living together, I noticed Brian cut out a page of the sports section of the local paper and made daily notations on it. One day, I asked him if it was some sort of crossword puzzle. He shot me a look, then nearly rolled on the floor with laughter as he said, "It's the sixty-four team bracket for March Madness!" Huh? I knew I needed to learn more about this secret sports world of Brian's.

Sharing your partner's passion isn't always easy, especially if you have an innate aversion to it. But at this point in the game, I realized that the heart of a Wabi Sabi artisan is a generous one. It is generous in the way that it sees its partner and in the way that it sees itself. It is generous by always giving the benefit of the doubt and seeing the other person's greatness beyond the scope of a momentary mess-up. A Wabi Sabi heart is generous in the interpretation of events and with its time and investment in making the relationship number one, despite opposing viewpoints.

Shopping is a great example of how couples who have a lot in common can still become diametrically opposed. Did you know that it has now been scientifically proven that men and women have radically different approaches to shopping? While women tend to troll the malls for deals and delight, men often apply a more linear methodology to purchases: go in, get it, and get out. According to research conducted by the University of Michigan School of Public Health, the reason lies in our evolutionary psychology.* Men hunt; women gather. Thousands of years ago women had to develop a keen sense of discernment to differentiate the poisonous berries from the nonpoisonous ones. At the same time, men planned their attack first in an effort to conserve energy, then grabbed their prey with practiced dexterity. These opposing strategies helped sustain the human race, but when it comes to consumer activity today, men and women often get entangled in a cross fire of their own making.

---

*D. J. Kruger and D. Byker, "Evolved foraging psychology underlies sex differences in shopping experiences and behaviors." Proceedings of the 3rd Annual Meeting of the NorthEastern Evolutionary Psychology Society, *Journal of Social, Evolutionary and Cultural Psychology* 3, no. 4 (2009): 328–42.

Like foraging the forest floor for nutrients, shopping is both a social and a sensual experience for women. A shared mission to search out the perfect little black dress can be a totally fulfilling night out with a favorite girlfriend. Women enjoy roaming around until something catches their eye, whether they are searching for clothes, shoes, purses, or accessories (especially if they are at bargain prices). One of the reasons women often (including me) adore shopping is that it fully engages all of our senses. Running your hand across the fabrics from silk and satin to linen and leathers, observing the colors and patterns and styles of the latest fashions, smelling the newest fragrances, and feeling fine leather shoes on your feet are delightful experiences most men never care about.

Those of you who struggle with your partner's passion for shopping—or with your partner's indifference to your own shopping obsession—may find inspiration in the way my friend Jerry occupies his time between his wife's fittings in the women's apparel department.

SHOP, PRAY, LOVE

Like many men I know, Jerry used to hate shopping, and luckily for him, his beloved wife, Diane, doesn't go shopping very often. However, on those rare occasions when she does hit the mall, she likes to have Jerry come along.

From the start, Jerry glanced at his watch frequently, making it obvious that he would rather not be there; in turn, Diane often felt pressured to rush through what used to be an enjoyable pastime.

One afternoon, as Jerry was anxiously biding his time while he sat in the middle of the dress department, he closed his eyes and literally asked God for help in dealing with what felt to him like an unbearable situation. Almost instantaneously, he received very clear and specific instructions: instead of waiting impatiently for their shopping expedition to end, he was to take out his pen and write Diane a love poem. Jerry followed this spiritual prompting, and as he did, he was overcome with a great sense of peace. Not only was he reconnecting with his love for Diane, but he had also made the shift from focusing on only his own preferences to a state of gratitude for the life they shared together. Rather than being bored and antsy, he became engaged and enlivened by discovering a different way to relate to the process of shopping altogether.

In the middle of this transformation, Diane came to show him a dress she wanted to buy and found Jerry sitting peacefully with a smile on his face. Confused but intent on shopping, she went back to trying on more clothes. After a brief interlude, she came back to check on him again.

He was still calm and peaceful. After she had made her purchases, she went to find him so they could finally leave before the experience inflicted any further damage. He asked her to sit down and said, "I'd like to share something with you."

Jerry quietly read her the beautiful love poem he had written as a tribute to her. She thanked him as her eyes filled with tears and the shutters on her heart blew wide open. They left the store giggling and holding hands in a bubble of love no shopping high could match. To this day, whenever they find themselves at a mall, Jerry writes her love poems.

But the story continues. Jerry's Wabi Sabi moment not only helped him and his wife; his epiphany helped a total stranger too.

One day Diane was in a department store, shopping with her mother. She saw a young woman quickly going through the clothing racks while a young man sitting nearby was looking miserable. Diane approached the man with a smile. "It's really horrible, isn't it?" she softly said to him.

"Yes," he said, dipping his head down as if not wanting to admit the torture he felt. "I really hate this."

"My husband used to feel this way too," Diane said. She surveyed the young man's face for a moment.

"Used to?" he asked, sitting up a little straighter.

Diane shared her story about how much Jerry hated shopping until he began using the time to write her these exquisite love poems.

The young man listened intently without saying a word. For a moment, he paused with a look of uncertainty on his face. Just as Diane drew back, hoping she hadn't overstepped her bounds, the young man leaped from his seat and called out to his wife who was closing in on the dressing room with an armful of clothes.

"Um, honey, do you have a pen?"

The Wabi Sabi wisdom of this story hardly needs explaining. Imagine hating a situation (shopping) so deeply that out of desperation all you can do is pray . . . and then to have your prayers answered instantly with a simple but brilliant solution. Our intuition feeds us the answers without fail when we take a moment to listen.

Whether it's basketball or accompanying your beloved to the mall, learning to love—or at least accept—what your partner loves requires an open mind and a generous heart. While I was struggling my way through the basics of learning about basketball (did they play in innings or quarters? Rebounds are good but traveling is bad?), I was fortunate enough to come across a book called *Secrets of a Very Good Marriage: Lessons from the Sea* by Sherry Suib Cohen. Sherry's heartfelt memoir opened my eyes to a new way of embracing Brian's favorite sport. Just as she embraced her husband, Larry's, love of the sea, Larry learned to get involved in Sherry's work as well. They both showed me that developing a passion for the things your mate is passionate about is one secret to a very happy marriage.

HOOK, LINE, AND ETERNAL LOVE

Bermuda. The very word conjures up images of pink sandy beaches surrounded by aquamarine waters and sun-drenched days melting into balmy evenings under star-speckled skies. What could be more romantic? This was the future on which Sherry's fantasy honeymoon with Larry was forecast.

Theirs had been a short but sweet courtship, and both were certain they were a match made in heaven. He was enchanted by her and said he knew the minute he saw her that they were meant to be together. She loved his zany sense of humor, as well as his honesty and his brilliance. It also didn't hurt that he was always game for anything.

They married and went to Bermuda for a much-anticipated honeymoon of rest, relaxation, and fun. What they got, however, was more than either of them bargained for. They shared an experience that would change the trajectory of their marriage, and their lives, forever.

After their crisp November wedding in New York, they arrived at the island paradise, excited to explore each other and their surroundings. On their first day Larry suggested to his new bride that they take out a rowboat, maybe do a little fishing and explore the islands that make up Bermuda. Sherry, a self-professed landlubber, had never been in a boat of any kind. The rickety old rowboat he heaved into the water gave her the chills. But, being very much in love and eager to please her new husband, she pushed aside her fearful thoughts of the sea and climbed into the small boat.

"It started off as a beautiful day . . . one that would be just me, Larry, and the sea. Lost in thought and in each other, we soon discovered we were lost at sea too!" To add to the excitement, the weather—which had started out sunny and warm—quickly turned cold and dreary. Sherry recalls how it began to rain. "I was trying to be a good sport. We rowed and rowed until finally, after what seemed like an eternity, we found our way back to shore."

As they stumbled off the boat, freezing cold, soaking wet, and exhausted, Larry saw a sign on the dock that said Fishing for Blues Tonight. Instantly rejuvenated and with the excitement of someone who had just won the lottery, he turned to his new bride and said:

"Let's go get warmed up, change our clothes, and then go fishing tonight!"

Her stomach sank. Her worst fears flooded her body as grim thoughts raced through her mind. Her life was *not* going to end in a dinghy.

This is not going to last. He is completely insane and off his rocker. After the day we just had, any normal person would want a long break from the ocean, she thought.

They didn't go fishing that night, or the next. But very quickly, Sherry began to understand how deeply connected Larry was to the ocean. She didn't really understand this passion and love for the sea but rationalized that maybe, in another life, he had been a great fisherman.

"I'm a very strong woman," she told me. "I know how to get my way and do what I want, *when* I want. But I also recognized that this was something I couldn't fool with. I knew, with absolute certainty, that for the rest of our life together the ocean would either be *with* us or *between* us. Realizing this, my choice became crystal clear."

Originally, Sherry saw Larry's immense love of the sea as his worst fault and a great potential threat to their relationship. But eventually she came to respect it and often wished she had something she loved as much. One day she had a beautiful epiphany when she realized she did love something as much as Larry loved the ocean: Larry himself! Larry is her greatest love.

"He is the smartest and funniest person I know. I love his wrinkles, the sag in his belly, the slight stoop to his walk. I would rather be alone with Larry in the middle of the ocean than any other place in the world."

Sherry eventually found enjoyment lying in the sun, or reading or writing while she spent time on the boat, but she never really came to love the ocean the way Larry does. Dealing with engine breakdowns is her least favorite boating experience; however, over the years she has even learned to bleed the engine when necessary and help navigate if the instruments fail.

WABI SABI PRINCIPLE

Play a part in your partner's life story. When you engage in your love's interests, you acknowledge not only the person, but also the passion.

Larry is a firm believer that a good marriage requires each person to be an active player in the other's stories, not just a passive bystander in them. Fortunately for Sherry, he has what it takes to put that philosophy into action. When Sherry is writing a magazine piece or a book, Larry accompanies her whenever possible. He has cooked with Paula

Deen and loudly admired Estée Lauder's paintings. He has even taken part in conflict-resolution sessions that were the basis of one of her books. "This way," Sherry says, "we each live colorful, layered lives. In fact, we each live two lives—together."

Inspired by Sherry's newfound appreciation and acceptance of Larry's fishing as well as his voluntary involvement in her passion for writing, I realized that my marriage would be well-served if I could find a way to love basketball, or at least love watching Brian doing what he loves. I was determined to embrace March Madness, that World Series of the college-basketball universe, with as much adoration as I could muster.

I decided that I would join Brian on the couch to watch the last fifteen minutes of any game he was watching. He was always delighted to answer my rookie questions, and he never got impatient with me when I called the end of the quarter "an inning." It was exciting to see the kid in him light up when he saw the players excel. By the time March Madness ended, I was looking forward to watching the last quarter of the NBA games he watched. But two more unexpected surprises emerged from my new practice of watching games with Brian: First, he began sharing more of his collegiate career memories with me, allowing me to appreciate and admire him in a whole new way. And second, I began to develop a genuine appreciation for the players as well as the game!

Don't get me wrong. I love Brian with all my heart and soul. But when I saw Avery Johnson, a suave point guard for the San Antonio Spurs (all five foot eleven of him), walk onto the court, I fell in love with him in a fanlike way. After a short while, he became my favorite player in the NBA. I can't explain it; I just became entranced with his wily ways on the hardwood. My other crush was Jason Kidd of the New Jersey Nets. Watching Avery and Jason work their magic gave me two more solid reasons to watch basketball with Brian.

The point is, you may never grow to love your partner's passion as much as he or she loves it, but you can grow your own heart by learning to love and support the things that really turn your partner on. One way I learned to connect to my "generous heart" is by taking five minutes to do a Heart Lock-In, a technique I learned from the Institute of Heartmath, which I find assists me in letting go of any negative emotions and reconnecting with my commitment to being a loving and supportive partner.

The heart is a muscle that pumps life-giving blood and oxygen throughout our bodies. We already know that running, biking, hiking, and other cardio workouts are proven ways to strengthen our hearts and improve our long-term health. In the same way, a Heart Lock-In improves the emotional and spiritual strength of your heart—only you don't have to break a sweat to reap the benefits!

For the past thirty years the visionaries at Heartmath, located in Boulder Creek, California, have studied the heart. Their research offers compelling evidence that the heart possesses its own intelligence and has great influence over how the body's many systems align themselves. The Heartmath scientists have found that when we focus on the area around the heart, while remembering and reexperiencing feelings such as love, appreciation, or gratitude, the positive results can immediately be measured in our heart rhythms (heart rate variability). They call this "heart coherence," a highly desirable state that improves our emotional, physical, and spiritual well-being.

Using the Heartmath techniques is one way to begin developing a generous and expansive heart. Just as your bicep muscles respond to lifting weights on a regular basis, spending time each day focused on the experience of love, appreciation, or gratitude builds a reservoir of these good feelings, which translates into greater love, joy, and harmony in your relationships. And quite frankly, who doesn't want more of that?

EXERCISE: *Strengthening Your Generous Heart Muscle*
(fill in the blanks)

What hobby, passion, or activity does your partner love that you have yet to embrace?

Use your imagination for just a moment, and ask yourself the following question: "If the key to having all my dreams come true is to find a way to fall in love with _____, what is the easiest way for me to do this?"

Now write down five or more ways your relationship would be improved if you could find a way to accept or possibly even love what your partner loves.

1 _____

2 _____

3 _____

4 _____

5 _____

Do a Heart Lock-In. It is about experiencing your heart at a deeper level.

Close your eyes and breathe slowly. Shift your attention away from your mind and focus on the area around your heart.

Remember the feeling of love or appreciation you have for your partner. Focus on this feeling for five to fifteen minutes.

Gently send that feeling of love or appreciation to yourself and to your partner.

(For a deeper experience of a Heart Lock-In, please visit www .wabisabilove.com/audio to download a guided audio version.)

With practice, a Heart Lock-In can provide physical, mental, and spiritual regeneration and resiliency so the next time you find yourself dreading something your partner loves to do, you can more easily make space for it. Growing your generous heart will also help grow your love for each other.

TWO

From Annoyed to Enjoyed

Ring the bells that still can ring. Forget your perfect offering. There is a crack in everything. That's how the light gets in.—*Leonard Cohen*

_____

While some experts might tell us not to sweat the small stuff, we all know it is the little things that can chisel away at even the best of relationships. Before those granular irks lead to the Big Bang in our partnerships, we need to develop relational safety nets to catch us before we fall. You can consider these strategies to be a quirk-turned-perk energy shift, if you will. A key aspect of Wabi Sabi is learning to move our focus from what makes our partners so annoying to what makes our partners so unique.

At its heart, this transition is about gratitude. Gratitude can be a marriage-saving emotion, especially if you tend to easily slide into feelings of annoyance about your partner's daily habits. Little rituals of thankfulness can sustain you as you struggle with the thing he or she did—*again*.

One of my favorite prayers comes from *A Course in Miracles*:

On this day where would you have me go?
What would you have me do?
What would you have me say and to whom?

For many years I began each day with this prayer as a way to center myself and receive divine guidance. It was particularly useful when I was feeling upset, stuck, or uninspired. I would follow this prayer by making a gratitude list that often looked like this:

Today I am grateful that I have fresh air to breathe and clean water to drink and for the many friends and family members who love me. I'm grateful that I have a healthy body, a creative mind, and interesting work. And before I got married, I usually added in the line "I am grateful for my soulmate who is on his way to spend his life with me."

So far so good. Then I got married and my prayers changed.

Dear God,
Help me. I have married a man who refuses to answer
the phone, but he will walk across a room to hand me the
phone so I can answer it.

Okay. I'm stretching the truth just a bit here, but like all couples, Brian and I each had quirks and odd behaviors that we had to learn to love and appreciate.

A daily practice of offering prayers of gratitude (whether you believe in a higher being or not) for your beloved mate—flaws and all—will keep your mind open and your heart receptive to remembering how much you love him or her. For it's really the *cracks* in our partners that we will someday miss the most.

MRS. LEE'S STORY

The cool, quiet room was overflowing with the grieving faces of friends and family as the funeral director invited Mrs. Lee up to the podium to speak.* The petite, elegant

---

*This story is based on a YouTube video that can be viewed at www.wabisabilove .com/video. It could not be determined whether this is based on a true character or not. The truthfulness of Mrs. Lee's words, however, overshadows the detail of fact or fiction.

widow walked slowly to the front of the small chapel and calmly began her eulogy.

"I am not going to sing praises for my late husband. Not today. Neither am I going to talk about how good he was." Mrs. Lee's eyes flashed.

"Enough people have done that here." She took a deep breath, allowing the air to fill her lungs before she continued. "Instead, I want to talk about some things that will make some of you feel a bit uncomfortable."

Several people stopped fanning themselves and sat up a little straighter. "First off, I want to talk about what happened in bed." She paused dramatically, shifting her weight from side to side. A crow cawed outside the chapel window. She watched it perch itself on a nearby tree.

"Have you ever had difficulty starting your car engine in the morning?" She carefully studied the faces about the room. With a loud, grinding sound, she snorted and rumbled, violently shaking her tiny frame.

"Well, that's exactly what David's snoring sounded like." A cough rose up from the center of the audience. "But wait," she continued. "Snoring wasn't the only thing." A few pairs of feet shuffled nervously under the chairs.

"There was also this rear-end wind action as well. Some nights it was so forceful, it would wake him up." A child giggled into her hand while her red-faced mother stifled a grin.

" 'What was that?' he would ask.

" 'Oh, it's the dog,' I would say. Patting his back and smoothing the covers, I would urge him to go back to sleep." She touched her hair as if remembering the way her hands felt as they placed themselves on her husband's gasping body. "Oh, you might find this very funny," Mrs. Lee offered the whisper of a smile. Her hands clutched the funeral program as she licked her dry lips. "But when his illness was at its worst, these sounds provided comfort and proof that my David was still alive."

Silence washed over the room. Even the birds outside seemed to be listening.

Mrs. Lee looked heavenward as her voice began to crack. "What I wouldn't give just to hear those sounds one more time before I sleep." A single tear wandered down her face, landing noiselessly on her lapel.

"In the end, it's these small things that you remember, the little imperfections that make them perfect for you.

"So, to my beautiful children," Mrs. Lee swept one hand toward the front row, "I hope that one day you, too, will find yourselves life partners who are as beautifully imperfect as your father was to me."

Mrs. Lee's eloquent tribute to her husband left the entire audience in tears. With just a few heartfelt words she summed up the mystery and magic of a lifelong marriage built on the foundation of love, imperfection, and acceptance that knows no bounds.

Wabi Sabi Love is grounded in acceptance. It's the practice of accepting the flaws, imperfections, and limitations—as well as the gifts and the blessings—that form your shared history as a couple. Acceptance and its counterpart, understanding, are crucial to achieving relationship harmony.

This is sacred love, not infatuation, or love that is convenient. What if we discovered that romantic love was never meant to be perfect, but to guide us to this highest form of love? What if, in fact, soulmate we-are-destined-for-one-another love exists to propel us into an understanding of Wabi Sabi Love, such as Mrs. Lee experienced?

Can you imagine what the world would look like, feel like, be like if the foundational premise of romantic love and deep intimacy were based on the art of loving one's imperfections rather than the illusionary fantasy that your relationship is fabulous only when each person is acting perfectly and behaving in ways that are acceptable to the other? Imagine a world in which imperfection is the accepted norm and is actually cherished.

Would the divorce rate drop? Would the love that brought us together alter the very way in which we relate to our partners? Would this new set of values provide an evolutionary segue into a love so perfectly imperfect that you learn to cherish that which used to drive you crazy?

Anyone who has found this highest level of Wabi Sabi Love knows that it comes in one way and one way only: through exploring, embracing, and actually falling in love with the cracks in each other and ourselves.

Sometimes the crack is a simple but persistent bad-hair day, an imperfection that one couple had to come to terms with.

BREAKTHROUGH WITH THE
UNTAMED MANE

According to Jan, Fred's wife of twenty-five years, Fred's hair is, in a word, unmanageable. Medium brown in color, it is wavy, curly, and very asymmetrical, sprouting out on both sides of his head.

"It's as if the sides of his head have different personalities," Jan claims. "It's so out of control that even a three-hundred-dollar professional haircut couldn't tame it."

The funny thing is, Fred is completely without vanity when it comes to his appearance. Before he met Jan, he was even known to buy eyeglasses without trying them on.

"I adore my husband," Jan says. "I've never met anyone less self-conscious about appearance than he is."

His attitude was quite a departure from what she had learned as a child. Growing up in a home with a father who was fastidious about his appearance and grooming, Jan consciously decided that she did not want to be her father's daughter. She doesn't wear makeup or high heels, and she chooses to keep her appearance as au naturel as possible. It is a trait that she and Fred definitely share. Fred, however, seems to take it to a much higher level of *naturalness* than Jan does.

"I'm an extraordinarily careless dresser," Fred admits. "I barely comb my hair, and most often you will find me in my uniform: sweat pants and a T-shirt underneath a flannel shirt."

Fred is a highly esteemed professor of psychology, a bestselling author and speaker who works from his home office.

"For years my wife has combed my hair, especially when I have to give a lecture. She gets irritated when I go out looking like a slob. When I'm in a particularly slothlike mode, she gives me the disapproving 'stare.'" By this, Fred is referring to the wilting glare that even his hair pays attention to. On some occasions, Jan swears she sees it shrink back in terror as she attacks it from all sides.

For many years Fred just endured Jan's attention to his wild head of hair. Some days he would tell her just to *"leave me alone*" while she would comb, brush, gel, or try to cut Fred's hair into submission.

"Like a stealth infiltrator, Jan even moved the hairbrush into the top drawer of my office desk one day so that she would have the brush handy when she wanted to fix my hair. It had lived happily in the bathroom for years."

Fred made many attempts to make peace with Jan's endless attention to his unruly mop, but gradually he realized that being annoyed wasn't useful. He loved his wife and understood that her intentions were both loving and pure. She really had his best interests at heart.

"We've both worked hard to stay present and connected in our marriage. I've come to an understanding that she's not changing. It was both grace and deep work to get from how *dare* she to how *care* she! Eventually, I realized that there's no one else who cares as much about me as she does. The brush represents her love for me," explains Fred.

Now, when Jan reaches for the brush, Fred no longer pulls away. He allows himself to experience the overarching kindness of this simple yet loving act. Most of the time he even says thank you to his deeply devoted and attentive wife.

And as for Jan, she has reached her own level of acceptance. "I've finally made peace with his total nonchalance about his appearance. In fact, I have even learned to respect his ability to stay true to himself."

The brush is staying in that top drawer, but why shouldn't it? Fred and Jan both know their love has actually been deepened by the very thing that once bristled more than just Fred's coiffure.

While we can't all be as unself-conscious as Fred about our appearance, I just love that he finally came to understand that Jan's love for him manifested in her efforts to spruce him up for his public appearances.

Many years ago I had my own Fred-like moment with a former boyfriend who wore an expensive suit and tie to work every day. One morning I saw a piece of lint on his shoulder, so I casually reached up to brush it away. You would have thought I was hauling off to smack him upside the head! He flinched and cast me a very nasty look. I quickly began to explain to him that I was only trying to remove some lint. He growled like the Incredible Hulk, then coolly replied, "Don't. Ever. Do. That. Again."

Was I missing something here? His reaction completely startled me. Up to this point he had been a very sweet and caring guy, but with one flick of my wrist (literally), he had morphed into a total jerk. When I asked him why he was suddenly so defensive, he admitted that his mother had always been "picking" at him and he just couldn't tolerate it. End of story. He was forty years old, acting fourteen, and refused to discuss it further. Luckily for me, the relationship ended quickly thereafter, but I learned an important lesson that has stayed with me to this day: it isn't always easy to find beauty and perfection in behavior that makes us crazy.

WABI SABI PRINCIPLE

Loving the quirks can be a perk when you see them as a part of the whole. Gratitude reminders help you see the Big Picture instead of dwelling on the details.

Another quirk-turned-perk couple I know has learned to view their idiosyncrasies as a part of their marital DNA.

LAUGHTER IS LOVE'S BEST MEDICINE

"We go together like 'chalk and cheese,'" says Deb, laughing, a beautiful British expat with royal lineage. Her husband, Ed, is from a working-class family in the Bronx, and while they are opposites in so many ways, they have been happily married for twenty-four years.

Their goal is first and foremost to be friends. When they have the occasional disagreement, they have learned how to let go and move on quickly.

"We are totally tuned in to each other," Ed explains. "If one of us insists on harping on something, the other simply says, 'I left that behind an hour ago.' It is our code for 'Let's move on.'"

For the past twenty years, however, Deb has found herself frustrated by something Ed does nearly every day.

Ed is a warm, outgoing, teddy-bear type of a guy who makes friends easily. In fact, he talks to nearly everyone with whom he comes in contact. Most would agree that this is a really wonderful quality to possess; for Deb, however, this trait can sometimes put a complete dent into her schedule.

"Ed loves to tell jokes, and he's really good at it. He shares his jokes with nearly everyone he meets, especially little children. The jokes are great the first time around, but I always end up waiting for him while he's busy entertaining strangers and innocent bystanders of all sizes and ages. After you've heard some of these jokes hundreds, maybe thousands of times, it can be pretty irritating."

Recently, Ed and Deb were standing in line at the bank when Ed struck up a conversation with the little girl behind them who was holding her mother's hand. She appeared to be around six years old and was wearing a yellow sundress. Ed said hello to the mother, made some small talk, and then kneeled down next to the little girl and said, "What did the baby strawberry say to its mother?"

The little girl, who turned to the folds in her mother's skirt, whispered shyly, "I don't know."

Ed replied, "The strawberry said to her mother, 'I'm in a jam!' "

And with that the little girl, her mother, and all the other people in line began laughing out loud.

Deb, not amused, realized that an open teller was available and nudged Ed to say good-bye so they could take care of business. As Deb walked over to the window, Ed figured he had just enough time for one more joke.

"Why is six afraid of seven?" He inserted a dramatic pause, then continued, "Because seven eight nine!"

Deb's familiar frustration crept up her neck like the tendrils of a vine on a post. She breathed deeply, slowly releasing the clutch on her paperwork as she slid it over the counter.

After they left the bank, they went to the local farmers market to pick up some fresh organic greens for a salad Deb was planning for lunch. Deb tried to shake off her irritation with some more deep breathing. The fresh air and vibrant vegetables helped calm her senses as she picked through some produce. As they approached a stand, amid the crowds they both noticed a little boy sitting on the curb. It was obvious that he was very bored as no one seemed to be paying him any attention. Ed walked over to the little boy and sat next to him on the curb, as Deb stood nearby.

"You look like a really smart little boy. Do you know what the right eye said to the left eye?" The boy shook his head.

" 'There's something that smells between us!' "

The little boy cast him a quizzical look. He scrunched his brow tightly as he considered what to make of Ed.

Not one for giving up easily, Ed was determined to coax a laugh out of the boy.

"How does a camel hide in the desert?"

Ears perked, the boy cocked his head to the right as he waited for the punch line.

"Camelflage!"

The little boy burst into a big belly laugh. Through Ed's kind gesture, the boy went from disinterested to merry in a single joke. In that moment, his harried-looking mom breathlessly approached them with a bagful of groceries. Before Ed had a chance to introduce himself and his wife, the little boy did the honors.

"Mom, meet Mr. Joke Man. He's really funny!"

She gave Ed a grateful smile, then collected her son to leave. As he took his mom's hand, the little boy waved good-bye before he disappeared into the crowd.

Deb was overcome. "In that moment I really got that this is Ed's essential nature. He just wants to make people happy with this special gift of his. I finally realized that irritating me was not his objective at all. Seeing that little boy light up like a Christmas tree, I finally understood that we can *really* make people happy. Ed didn't just give that little boy a gift that day. He gave me one too."

You can go from "annoyed" to "enjoyed" by just one small Wabi Sabi shift in perception. Imagine how much more fun and rich all our relationships would be if each time we found ourselves "annoyed," we made it a personal practice to stop for a moment, take a deep breath, and see if we would be *willing* to find a way to get to "enjoyed." The simple act of being *willing* can open up a new world of possibility.

For instance, being on time in Brian's world means being ten minutes early—something he learned from his years as an athlete, where coaches have zero tolerance for tardiness. In my world, being on time means I am never more than five minutes late. That fifteen minute differential was often the cause of many a tense moment when we first got together. One day, as we were getting ready to go to the airport on a trip, I noticed that Brian's suitcase was at the front door and he was calmly sitting in the living room watching TV, while I was standing in the bathroom, putting on my makeup, rushing, stressed out, and sweating. I realized that if I had started getting ready a few minutes earlier, I'd be much happier and more relaxed and my hair wouldn't be wilting from perspiration.

Luckily, Brian has come to accept my tendency to rush about last minute, just as I have learned to appreciate his more planned and placid approach. While either one of us could have faulted the other for our differing styles, we've chosen to view them as one small part of an overall great package.

We all know it's the little things that add up to that Great Big Thing that can destroy our partnerships. A willingness to embrace even the oddest of discrepancies can forge relationships based on unconditional love; and who cares if your kitchen floor takes a bit of a beating in the process?

LOVE LESSONS FROM THE KITCHEN FLOOR

Even though Diane truly loved Jerry, she was confronted on a daily basis with something about him she found very hard to embrace: his passion for poppy-seed bagels. Since childhood, Jerry has had a love affair with this particular snack, and, in fact, he enthusiastically devours one nearly every day. Jerry slices and toasts his bagel, then takes it into his home office to relish its flavor.

But like Hansel in the fairy tale, Jerry always leaves a trail of poppy seeds that sweeps across the white kitchen floor, through the center of the house, and into his office. Jerry is aware that he is a bit of a "sloppy Joe." Although he often makes an effort to clean up the poppy seeds, his cleaning skills somehow never match Diane's desire to have an utterly spotless floor.

One day Diane was feeling uncharacteristically grumpy. As she entered the kitchen and looked down, her level of grumpiness increased a hundredfold when she found herself swimming in a sea of scattered poppy seeds yet again.

As she had done a thousand times before, Diane moistened a hand towel and got down on her hands and knees to begin cleaning up the mounds of accumulated seeds.

Just once, she thought, *I would like to come into the kitchen and not find these poppy seeds*, huffing as she vigorously hand-wiped the floor to her satisfaction.

As she sat back on her heels, a thought struck her through the haze of her own frustration. *What if the floor never had any more poppy seeds on it?*

As if hit by lightning, Diane suddenly realized *that would mean there would be no more Jerry!*

Tears flooded her eyes as she stood up. She gazed down at the poppy seeds that were gritting up her floor. Instead of looking like grains of gray sand, they suddenly looked amazing to her—like little black diamonds that represented everything in her life that was precious and sacred to her.

She rushed into Jerry's study, threw her arms around him, and kissed him through tears of joy. He gave her a quizzical yet loving look as he popped the last bit of poppy-seed bagel into his mouth, then brushed the seeds that had landed on his shirt onto the floor.

Today she describes it this way: "Now, no matter how many seeds I may mop up, I'm very peaceful inside. Whenever I see those poppy seeds, they fill me with so much love and gratitude; and on some days I deliberately leave them and my old compulsive behavior behind as I smile, turn on my heel, and walk away."

We all have our unique ways of responding to life. Learning the ways of our beloveds requires paying attention to all the ways they make decisions and respond to life's challenges. Chances are they don't do things exactly the way we would do them (and who is to say our way is the right way or the only way?), so I suggest you recite the prayer of a Wabi Sabi relationship to yourself often. It is the Serenity Prayer:

> *God, grant me the serenity to accept the things I cannot change, courage to change the things I can, and wisdom to know the difference.*

Whether it's your mate's bad hair, bad jokes, or poppy seeds that get under your skin, remember the prayer of a

Wabi Sabi relationship before you go ballistic. With that in mind, try this simple exercise to test your ability to go from "annoyed to enjoyed."

EXERCISE: *Learning to Go from Annoyed to Enjoyed*

All that's required to make this shift in perception is the realization that you have the power to see your mate's behavior through a new, gentler, and kinder lens. Often when we are annoyed, we are holding a righteous position. We believe our way is the *right* way and our partner's way is the *wrong* way—a surefire method for inviting stress and tension into our relationships.

PART ONE: Select one of your partner's behaviors that really drives you crazy:

(For example: my wife criticizes me, or my husband contradicts how I discipline the kids.)

Write down 5–10 times or situations when this behavior has surfaced:

1 _____

2 _____

3 _____

4 _____

5 _____

6 _____

7 _____

8 _____

9 _____

10 _____

Answer these questions:

How many more times am I willing to allow this situation to annoy me? _____

What payoff do I get by finding fault in my partner?

_____

What does being "annoyed" keep me from having?

_____

Where did I learn to be annoyed by other people's behavior?

_____

PART TWO: Imagine that your mate's annoying behavior exists solely to teach you how to become a more loving, compassionate person, and write down three gifts of the behavior.

1 _____

2 _____

3 _____

Looking for the gifts is an invaluable skill in a world in which we can't control people's behavior. While our partners may never change the quirks and idiosyncrasies that we find maddening, we can change our perceptions of them.

Deb learned that Ed's need to share his humor brought more happiness to the world and to her. Fred finally realized that Jan's attention to his hair was a sincere expression of her love and care for him. To Diane, Jerry's daily sprinkling of poppy seeds on the kitchen floor became a symbol of her deep love and appreciation of him and his blessed presence in her life. They made the necessary mind shift to go from annoyed to enjoyed to joy!

If you're having a hard time finding your joy, know that you always have a choice. In fact, when it comes to creating Wabi Sabi Love, the power of choice is your closest ally.

THREE

Wabi Sabi Choices

Ever since my house burned down, I see the moon
more clearly.—*Gregory Colbert*

Remember that old TV commercial that showed various
people making bad food choices after which they would
smack themselves on the forehead and exclaim, "I could
have had a V8!"? I haven't seen it for years, but I still think
about that commercial when faced with everyday decisions.
As creatures of habit, we often operate on autopilot, acting
in ways that were instilled in us by our surroundings or our
culture and forgetting that we have the power to choose.
Routines can easily become ruts, and unless we're willing
to become more flexible in our thinking, we may find ourselves stuck in them for years.

Eight-year-old Nancy was hanging out in the kitchen, helping her mom prepare the Sunday pot roast. Sundays and pot roast had been a family tradition for as long as Nancy could remember.

"Mom, how come you are cutting off both ends of the pot roast before placing it in the baking pan?" Nancy asked.

Her mother thought about it for a few moments and then said, "That's the way your grandmother always did it, but I'm not sure why."

A few minutes later the doorbell rang, announcing the arrival of Grandma and Grandpa.

Nancy excitedly ran to the door to let them in and quickly grabbed her grandmother by the hand, leading her into the kitchen.

"Grammy, why do you cut off both ends of the pot roast before putting it in the pan?"

Her grandmother sat down and tried to remember. Finally she said, "That's how my mother taught me to prepare a pot roast. Let's give her a call and ask her."

Nancy and her grandmother called the nursing home to speak to her great grandmother.

When they asked her the question, she began to laugh and said, "I had to cut off both ends of the pot roast in order to make it fit into the only baking pan I had."

Because we are creatures of habit, we often do things the way we have always done them, believing that our way is the right way. Then we meet and marry people who have grown up with entirely different sets of habits and behaviors who also believe that theirs is the right way to do things. And that's how trouble starts. We bring our assumptions, fantasies, and memories into a marriage with our "right way" and "wrong way" radar on high. We have opinions on everything, from the direction the toilet paper should roll to whether to clean the kitchen as we cook or wait to handle the mess later. One of us believes kitchen countertops are there to hold every possible appliance for our convenience, while our partner believes the counters should be as clean and clear as possible. We think that a towel can be reused for five days; our partner insists on a fresh towel after every shower. (And let's not even get started about whether or not the wet towel belongs on the floor next to the hamper.)

The crazy thing is that most of us never realize that we have the ability to *question* our beliefs and habits. As human beings, we have the magnificent capacity known as *choice*. We can choose at any moment to make new choices about our beliefs, habits, and ways of doing things. But instead of exercising this choice, many of us fault our partners and rapidly slide into judgment, criticism, or resentment.

There is an easy solution to this issue. The next time you are about to fault your partner, ask yourself three questions: Why do I think he is wrong? When did I learn this? What will happen if I give up my position (that my partner is wrong) and just let it go?

THE ANTIDOTE TO "SHOULDING" ON YOUR MATE

They met at a book-signing party at UCLA thirty years ago. Barnet was instantly taken with Sandi's passion, beauty, and strength, and although Sandi had come to the event with someone else, she was very intrigued by Barnet's intellect, wit, and charm. "I immediately got her phone number, took her to dinner the next day, spent the night, and never left," is how Barnet remembers their meeting. Two days later he heard a voice in his head that said, "Do not play games with this woman. Do not do your usual thing." Having earned a reputation as a bit of a player when it came to women, Barnet made a silent pledge to himself not to do anything to consciously hurt this woman who had stopped him in his tracks.

They married eighteen months later and within eight years had a daughter, a dog, and a home in Studio City, California. Barnet, a writer/filmmaker, worked from home, while Sandi quickly rose up the corporate ladder as a specialist in the fashion industry. Her work was often complex, stressful, and demanding.

Even though they were deeply committed to each other, they had their share of arguments and tumultuous outbursts. "But we were always interested in exploring personal growth and alternative health options," explains Sandi. "Early on, we learned how to meditate. We saw meditation as both a spiritual path and a tool for staying healthy."

Ironically, meditation also became the fire starter of frequent arguments. The scenario went something like this: Sandi would often arrive home later than she expected (thanks to L.A.'s notorious traffic) and stressed out from a difficult day at work. She would be tired, grumpy, and in need of some TLC. Overwrought and discombobulated, she would begin to download her nightmare of a day on Barnet. Armed and ready, he'd be standing with his left foot forward, right hand on his hip, replying in a righteous, authoritative voice.

"But, Sandi . . . did you *meditate* today?" Infuriated, her standard response became:

"I have no time to meditate. *You* work from home. You can meditate all day if you'd like. But I have an office to get to."

And then they were off and running down the same nasty track where Barnet tried to solve her problems, while

Sandi wasn't sure he understood them at all. She resented his know-it-all attitude, and he felt hurt and neglected that she wouldn't heed his sound advice. Barnet remembers that every time he'd remind her of the stress-reducing benefits of meditation, she would single out the word *stress*, turn her hands into fists by her side, and become red in the face.

Barnet explains, "Back then, whenever Sandi wasn't 'okay,' I wanted to fix her. It seemed reasonable to me that if she would take the time to meditate, she wouldn't end up so stressed out. Underneath that, of course, was my own fear and insecurity that something was wrong with me if I couldn't make her happy."

What Sandi wanted to come home to was a man who'd embrace her and then thoughtfully listen to her and allow her to vent the frustrations of her day without making her feel inadequate. What they came to see through some serious work was that different visions of what it meant to be a couple were causing their fights.

Now, on the days when Sandi comes home in a tizzy, less frequent though they are, Barnet comes from a stronger place of understanding, realizing that she wants to be heard, not fixed.

And on days when Barnet reverts back to that position of left foot forward, right hand on his hip, and a righteous, authoritative voice, Sandi simply stands in front of him, her left foot forward, right hand on her hip in response. They call this "the Stance," which is their code for the recognition that some old, ineffective behaviors have surfaced and need to be released.

"The whole energy shifts and we laugh and laugh . . . at ourselves, at each other . . . and then we effortlessly move into something that is fun," says Sandi. "Fun is one thing we have in abundance now."

WABI SABI PRINCIPLE

Being a Wabi Sabi couple means to give and receive, not just dump and vent.

As demonstrated in this story, Wabi Sabi communication isn't always about words. Have you ever noticed what happens in your own body when you're trying to be nice, but inside you're really seething? Or when you think you are controlling your anger only to find that your words don't match what your body is saying?

Barnet and Sandi have found a simple and yet brilliant way to quickly and deeply communicate nonverbally. It's that kind of connection that keeps us in communion with each other. Whether we realize it or not, we all intuitively pick up on our partners' nonverbal cues to their world. It's up to us to choose to pay attention to the true message behind the words and to then provide what Brian calls "a deep level of care."

The choices we make impact our relationships. Whether it's the way we speak, how we communicate with our bodies, or what we decide to accept or let go, choice is at the center of everything we do. German philosopher Rainer Maria Rilke once said, "A good marriage is one in which each partner appoints the other to be the guardian of his solitude, and thus they show each other the greatest possible trust." Sometimes we are required to dig deep before we decide to surrender our childhood fears in order to establish that "greatest possible trust," as my friend Robin did.

WABI SABI OR WAR

Growing up with a single mom, Robin always recognized the one telltale sign that things were either okay or not okay for everyone: the state of the kitchen. If it was clean, all was well. If it was dirty—and sometimes dirty dishes were stacked high—her mom wasn't coping. That meant nothing was going to go right for anyone.

It was natural, then, for Robin to make a clean kitchen the priority when she became a single mom. As soon as she could afford it, she moved into a lovely water-view home with white walls, large windows, and a modern, open-space kitchen. Her children lived with her every other week, and even though on the "kids' week," things got somewhat messy, never, ever were there stacks of dirty dishes. When they took off, she would clean high and low. The house reflected the state of mind she preferred: simple, elegant, and with a lovely breeze moving through. She felt very free and light.

When her beloved Brian moved in, all heaven broke loose. Her two kids returned to live with her full time, along with a dog. To add to an already lively household, Brian's college-age kids often visited with friends. Brian had lived a good bit of his life in the backwoods of West Virginia, heating his house with a wood stove and driving three miles to the nearest paved road. So the furniture he brought was very Wabi Sabi—including a huge old dinner table from his parents' house (it replaced Robin's glass and metal-weave dining-room set), an oversize coffee table that had been with him since his younger years of living in Bogotá, Colombia, and a lot of pictures that were outfitted in various unmatched plain wooden frames. Even the garage went from an echoing cavern for a single mom's car to everything a professional forester, outdoor enthusiast, and organic gardener could need. Every time she looked at the kayaks, compost buckets, and turkey smoker, she had to smile. She knew she was faced with a choice: it was either Wabi Sabi or war. If it was true love, she could move from controlled, clean, and clear to finding order in the midst of chaos.

The greatest challenge, of course, was the kitchen. Brian is a talented organic cook who borders on gourmet, and the moment he moved in, the kitchen became his. Overnight they had Mason jars for drinking glasses and every kind of strange mismatched container on the counters for spices and staples. He bought "scratch and dent" items from the discount store and left food in the refrigerator three times longer than Robin might have. Worst of all, while she had cooked using a pan and spatula one time a day, he used a wide range of pots, pans, dishes, and utensils to prepare their three squares a day.

To calm her heart and mind, Robin repeated "Wabi Sabi or war" frequently as she would make her contribution of cleaning up after meals. But underneath, she wondered, *Where is my sanity? Where did my fresh breeze go? Where can I go to find my serene state of mind?*

Then one day, something happened. Everyone was in the kitchen, Brian was making a mess, the kids were spilling chips and salsa and drinks, and Robin suddenly saw her new life for what it truly was: full of love. When seen through the lens of Wabi Sabi Love—which she had chosen as her adult reality in place of her more difficult childhood reality—the messy kitchen was no longer a symptom of dysfunction but rather a symbol of a loving family. Seeing everyone laughing and having a great time in the midst of the flurry, Robin suddenly realized she had a choice about shifting her view of it all, and she did. Clean was not the only expression of sane, and the mess itself wasn't evidence of a neurosis. Quite the contrary! It was evidence of a happy family. This new truth took root within her, and, finally, she joined in the fun. Wabi Sabi won her over in that moment, and it's had her ever since.

Robin's choice to shift her perspective from "chaos in the kitchen" to "love, laughter, and happiness in the home" is Wabi Sabi at its best. Letting go of her inner child's need for order in the kitchen allows her to fully embrace the warm, loving family for which she has become the cherished and beloved matriarch.

EXERCISE: *Putting On a New Cloak*

As kids, we used to play dress-up, slipping in and out of roles as easily as we slid into and out of our flip-flops. It didn't really matter which roles we chose as long as everyone got to play one. As adults, however, we have grown attached to the roles we play and the beliefs that sustain them.

In this exercise you will practice putting on a magic cloak to observe the art of viewing the circumstances of your life through a slightly different filter.

Sit down by yourself with a pad and pencil. Write down a few things that really annoy you about your partner. Examples might be leaving the toilet seat up or down; squeezing the toothpaste tube in the middle or at the end; leaving drawers and cabinets half open; or sleeping with the window shut.

Close your eyes and imagine you own a magic cloak that has the power to shine a positive light on negative situations. As you place the imaginary cloak over your shoulders, call to mind one of your partner's so-called annoying habits.

Now challenge yourself creatively, and see how many interesting, amusing reasons you can make up to explain why your partner commits such acts. "She squeezes the toothpaste tube in the middle because it comes alive if you touch the end" or "He leaves the drawer open so the little elves that live under the stove can hop back in when we're not looking!"

Open your eyes and take a few deep breaths.

Write a new fairy tale to explain the behavior to replace the recurring horror movie you keep replaying in your mind.

Last, commit to trying on your partner's behavior yourself. You will undoubtedly meet with internal resistance, and you may never learn to love doing it yourself. The point is to allow yourself to feel what it is like to walk in your partner's shoes, or should we say, flip-flops?

(For a deeper experience of this exercise, please visit www.wabi sabilove.com/audio to download a guided audio version.)

Changing just one thing about the way we look at the world can alter our entire perception. The way we choose to see things, whether positively or negatively, impacts our relationships in so many ways. A Wabi Sabi choice offers new avenues for seeing the world differently and influences not only what we say, but *how* we say it. Wagging a finger will elicit a different response than offering a hand. Either way, the choice is up to each of us as to which way the cookie crumbles and if we laugh, yell, or cry when it does.

FOUR

Humor and Humility

Words are, of course, the most powerful drug used
by mankind.—*Rudyard Kipling*

Until I met Brian, I had always assumed I had a good sense
of humor. I love to laugh (who doesn't?), and I am a big
fan of silly humor that triggers uncontrollable fits of laughter. You could say I am an *easy laugh,* because I'll giggle at
almost anything even closely related to funny. When I met
Brian, however, I was devastated to learn there is humor I
just don't understand.

As someone who is considered a very funny guy by those
who know him best, Brian has an irreverent, sophisticated

type of humor that slides by my intellect on most occasions. Often Brian says something dry, witty, or teasing and
it sails right over my head and into outer space. Over time
he figured out that he needed to preface his witticisms with
"this is meant to be funny," which proved to be very useful
for my black-and-white way of processing things.

On a flight from New York to San Diego we found ourselves seated next to a guy who was reading a book while
continuously laughing out loud. At one point when he was
nearly doubled over with spasmodic gasps, I tapped him on
the shoulder so I could get in on the joke. With tears running down his face, he handed me the book and managed
to blurt out: "Read these two pages."

With Brian looking over my shoulder, we began to read
from the book *Letters from a Nut* by Ted L. Nancy, with an
introduction by Jerry Seinfeld. By the third line in, we were
laughing so hard our sides hurt. (It's rumored that Seinfeld actually wrote the book and made up the name Ted L.
Nancy, but no one seems to know for sure.) We finished the
two pages, then wiped our eyes with our sleeves. Through
our tears of laughter, we looked at each other and suddenly
stopped midchuckle. We couldn't believe it. At thirty thousand feet we had actually found common comedic ground!

That day we discovered we are both major Jerry Seinfeld
fans. In fact, Brian had seen Seinfeld more than a dozen

times. Now, at least once a year we have a standing date to see Seinfeld live onstage, and together we laugh until we cry.

WABI SABI PRINCIPLE

Laughter is not only the world's best medicine. It is also the glue that lightens difficult moments and acts as a delicious bonding agent.

Laughter not only heals; it also brings people closer together. There is nothing more heartwarming and connective than a hearty belly laugh shared with those you love. As you will see in this next story, small moments of humor can make way for big doses of intimacy.

GRUMPINESS CURE: A PINCH OF HUMOR

What happens when a hermit marries a social butterfly? Gay is an intellectual who likes to socialize in what he calls "small homeopathic doses." He's really comfortable spending big chunks of time alone. Katie, who is brilliant and very accomplished as well, is very much a social butterfly. In between teaching workshops around the globe and running their institute, she loves to dance, party, and have as much fun as possible.

Quite often in the early days of their marriage, Gay would be working at his desk, locked into his head, and Katie would come in and interrupt him with some random thought, feeling, or idea, or—as Gay explains it—"something quite trivial." Gay found her intrusions unnecessary and annoying and would usually say something to derail her, such as, "Can't you see I am doing very important work right now?"

This situation, which repeated itself often, created disharmony and tension between the two of them "the first five hundred times it happened," Gay jokingly remembers.

One day Katie took a slightly different approach. When she interrupted him, Gay launched into his usual "Can't you see . . ."

And Katie's response, which she offered with an exaggerated tone of reverence, was:

"Thank you, Professor Number 435. I would have never been able to figure that out by myself!"

Gay laughed so hard he almost fell over.

During his twenty years as a professor of clinical psychology at the University of Colorado, his official psychologist license number was 435.

Now, whenever Katie walks into Gay's office to interrupt him while he's hard at work, Gay responds with a greatly exaggerated persona: "Can't you see I was just about to crack the secrets of the Universe?" To which Katie replies with some version of: "Thank you, Professor Number 435. I would have never been able to figure that out by myself!"

Knowing when to use humor and when to back off has served Katie well.

But unless you're a professional onstage comedian, humor can't be the cure-all for every situation. For those times when you've hit a bump in the road and the shit has hit the fan, you are in the heat of an upset, in breakdown, or out of sorts with yourself or with each other, it will help immensely to realize that you are in the middle of a Wabi Sabi moment. Invite the concepts of Wabi Sabi to join you. Know that you're being challenged to find the irony, the absurdity, or the ultimate insignificance of the conflict at hand. Sometimes creating code names for each other, as I mentioned in the introduction, can diffuse the anxiety of the situation. So when Brian sees me wagging my finger with my head cocked just so, I know he's going to call me Sheila any minute. When he's condescending, you better believe I shout *Wayne!* from across the room.

If that doesn't work, getting some distance can help. For me, taking the time to meditate, practicing an emotional-release technique, or even taking a brief walk around the corner to clear my head (so I don't shake it at Brian) helps me move toward letting go of the emotional turbulence that is part and parcel of any long-term relationship. It gives me the necessary distance and perspective to look at things in a new way. Then I can begin to appreciate the crack and open my mind to see and feel other solutions, some of which might be foreign to my usual ways of thinking.

Just to be clear, I'm not asking you to pretend or ignore real issues that need to be dealt with, but rather to find what is perfect about your relationship's imperfections. This is the essence of Wabi Sabi that invites creative solutions to emerge through the cracks.

A TALE OF LEARNING TO TRUST

Joan and Gordon were recently married and madly in love when they decided to visit the Oaxaca Coast in Mexico. Both highly educated and accomplished, these two baby boomers shared many of the same intellectual and spiritual pursuits. However, when it came to food, they couldn't have been more different.

Joan doesn't care much about food other than as a means to fuel her body, while Gordon loves everything about shopping, preparing, and eating food. Joan can be happy with a slice of melted cheese on a piece of pita. Gordon wants freshly baked multigrain baguettes with freshly picked and diced heirloom tomatoes drizzled with the finest extra virgin olive oil.

However, when Joan does get hungry and her blood sugar drops, she has to eat immediately. Instantly. Pronto. RIGHT *NOW*.

So, there they were in the lovely coastal town of Huatulco. They took a taxi from their hotel to a restaurant on the water that they believed would provide a delicious meal. The sun was just beginning to set as the taxi dropped them off; they walked down the stairs to the beach to find the restaurant . . . which was closed . . . because it was Sunday. They walked back up the stairs in the dimming twilight, and, of course, the taxi was long gone and the street was deserted.

Joan's blood sugar had suddenly dropped, and she needed to eat immediately so they went to the first restaurant they found, which was very fancy. Gordon was not impressed and didn't want to eat there. He wanted to walk one more block to find another place. But Joan was insistent that she had to eat RIGHT NOW because she was about to pass out. They entered the fancy place, sat down, and, sure enough, had a very expensive, lousy meal.

When they left the restaurant, they discovered a darling pizzeria they could have eaten at and enjoyed so much more for a lot less money right around the corner.

The next morning Gordon was still steaming about the previous night. While he and Joan had breakfast, he told her that he wished he could have just ignored her and walked one more block to find a more suitable place to eat. Grateful that at least she didn't have to walk far for her breakfast, Joan cast him a look as if to say, "This is a physiological issue I have dealt with all my life. Get used to it."

"Are you familiar with the mythological Greek poet Orpheus?" he asked her.

"Who?" she said, stuffing a large piece of bread into her mouth.

Gordon began to tell her the story.

Back in olden times, Orpheus was in love and married to a beautiful nymph named Eurydice. Eurydice ran into a nest of snakes, one of which bit her fatally on her heel.

Distraught at the death of his love, Orpheus sang so mournfully that all the nymphs and gods wept. On their advice, Orpheus traveled to the underworld to bring Eurydice back to life. Through his music, he softened the hearts of Hades and Persephone (he was the only person ever to do so), who agreed to allow Eurydice to return with him to earth, but on one condition: he must walk in front of her and not look back until they both had reached the upper world. He was instructed that no matter how much she cried or protested, Orpheus must not look at her or pay heed to her or he would lose her forever.

They began up the stairway to the upper world. Eurydice asked him to turn around and give her one kiss, but Orpheus knew that he shouldn't listen to her. He knew best. She continued to plead and beg for him to turn around and look at her. Eventually, against his better judgment, he turned around to her most plaintive plea only to catch a glimpse of her disappearing forever.

As Gordon finished his story, he looked across the breakfast table at his beloved Joan.

"Having heard that story, how does that make you feel?" he asked her.

"It makes me feel like punching you in the face," Joan said, swallowing the last of her delicious breakfast.

Gordon leaned back in his chair, laughing hysterically, and then Joan—in concert—began to laugh as well.

They now refer to this as their Huatulco Moment. After all these years, it still generates a good laugh between them. Gordon has since truly recognized Joan's need to eat frequently and now insists that Joan never leave home without a PowerBar in her pocketbook.

As this story illustrates, Gordon was able to transform his annoyance (and a potentially lifelong grievance) by utilizing his knowledge of a classic myth to express his love and support to Joan. I love this story because he was saying,

"I will go to hell and back for you, but if you want to share this life together, you have to trust me to guide you." Wow! Now, that is a man who knows how to put his sword in the ground and stake his claim. Bravo.

As someone who also suffers from low-blood-sugar issues, I understand that intense "feed me now before I die" feeling that Joan described. Like Gordon, Brian often reminds me to make sure I have a bag of almonds nearby to keep me on an even keel so those punch-in-the-face moments never even come up.

WAYS TO ADD HUMOR

As you know, Brian and I learned early on in our relationship to use code names to put ourselves, and each other, on notice when our behavior was becoming less than attractive.

Creating silly nicknames is another playful way to handle potentially tough situations. For instance, if your partner is always hogging the blankets, you could name him or her "blanket monster," which would be code for *I need you to share.*

My friend Jim calls his wife, Jackie, "the kleptophoniac" because even though they have five portable phones in their three-story house, she is always walking off with them and he can never find a phone when he needs one.

This is meant to be a playful way to keep each other in check while communicating you mean business, so don't let it turn into unpleasant name-calling.

Or perhaps write your beloved a theme song. Take the melody of a song or well-known jingle such as "You Are My Sunshine" or the Oscar Mayer hot dog jingle or any little ditty that you like. Then rewrite the words to tell your partner how much you love him and his little quirks. Regardless of whether you have a beautiful singing voice or not, sing him his theme song. Often.

Brian frequently makes me special CDs filled with songs that describe how he feels about me. One of my favorites is the Billy Joel tune "Just the Way You Are," because it expresses the principles of Wabi Sabi Love so beautifully. When we love each other just the way we are, we are free to be who we are without pretense, anxiety, or shame.

HUMILITY

Another key concept to understand as you build your Wabi Sabi relationship is humility. As humans, we don't seem to come naturally to humility. When an issue arises, it's only human nature to think that the cause of the problem is over *there*. Not many of us were trained by our parents to reflect upon our judgments and true motivations. When humor, metaphor, or mythology aren't appropriate avenues to resolving a situation, sometimes a big dose of humility does the trick.

VEGAN + HUNTER = SACRED UNION

A beautiful, high-energy, flirtatious woman, Jill truly believed that her perfect mate would be someone who would share her interest in yoga, meditation, spirituality, metaphysics, and all things organic, including her vegetarianism. With a great deal of angst and trepidation, Jill left California and returned to her home in New Jersey. She soon found herself engaged to Ray, a duck-hunting, meat-eating, motorcycle-riding, cigarette-smoking "guy's guy." He was also a bit socially phobic and preferred to stay home most of the time.

With all of her heart, Jill desperately wanted Ray to be The One. But there was a major obstacle in the way. She definitely believed she was the "consciously evolved one" in their relationship and found herself in near constant judgment of his habits, hobbies, and behaviors. We all know how well judgment and nagging criticism sits with someone.

Eventually Jill broke up with Ray, explaining to him that she needed to find someone with whom she had more in common. Ray was still loving, kind, and understanding, even though Jill was breaking his heart.

"If this is what you need to do, I will accept your decision, but I will wait for you no matter how long it takes," he said.

During this time they continued to live together as roommates because neither of them could afford to sell the house they shared. Ray treated Jill as he always had, with deep care, respect, and love. Jill began to clearly see that while Ray always loved her unconditionally, her love had been extremely conditional, judgmental, and rigid in the way she treated him. She also realized that most of the "spiritual" guys she dated talked a good talk that rarely translated into actions. Ray, on the other hand, was kind, authentic, loyal, and compassionate. He had all of the qualities that Jill considered "spiritual." Always putting her needs first and showering her with adoration, Ray had the ability to make her feel special, and this was something she realized she had taken for granted.

Slowly, she began to see him with new eyes. By observing him in close quarters over a period of five months, she was able to see and feel his nonjudgmental approach to life, and she realized that she'd been acting spiritually arrogant, believing she was the "teacher." Ray's ability to love her unconditionally and let her be herself showed her that he was really a teacher to her. It was a humbling moment for her.

Jill had always fancied herself a true nature lover, gardening and composting to her heart's delight, but one afternoon when Ray returned from hunting, he shared with her his experience of reverence for the beauty of the woods, the sky, the smells, and the silence he experienced. In astonishment, she saw something that surprised her and really opened up her heart—there are so many different and beautiful ways to commune with nature, not just her way!

A few days later Ray asked Jill to go with him to the funeral of his former boss, Bob. More than 350 bikers were in attendance, but none of Ray's former colleagues would stand up to pay tribute to Bob. Ray put his fears aside, walked calmly to the front of the chapel, and shared from his heart what a well-loved and good man Bob was. It was at this moment as Jill sat mesmerized, watching him overcome his social phobia, the one thing she most judged about him, that she truly fell in love with Ray. His ability to speak from his heart and comfort Bob's family made her discover a new level of respect for Ray. She had never felt more proud of him.

After four years of an on-again, off-again engagement, the wedding date was finally set. Jill has found the love and the peace of mind she had been searching for all those years.

Jill and Ray's story reminds me of one of my favorite quotes: "It's a both/and world. It's both the way you say it is and the way I say it is." Jill's particular point of view on "spirituality" limited her ability to see and appreciate Ray's innate spiritual nature. She had judged his shyness, which is so unlike her outgoing personality, until fortunately she was able to witness Ray's brave, loving, and compassionate side at the funeral.

While she used to deem Ray's soft-spoken nature as unacceptable, she now saw it as one of his most attractive and lovable attributes. Jill experienced a true Wabi Sabi shift that has allowed her to fully love and admire Ray in ways she never imagined.

WAYS TO ADD HUMILITY

Jill had blocked her heart from receiving Ray's love because she had made the assumption that her beliefs and behaviors made her the more "spiritual" one, which caused her to distance herself from him. The exercise below will help you leave your assumptions behind by practicing what Harvard psychologist Ellen Langer calls "mindful awareness."

Pick a time when you can observe your partner for five minutes without being too obvious (you don't want to make him or her self-conscious). During this time you want to look for five things that are different from the last time you really noticed him or her. The fact is, people grow and change all the time, but often we're too busy to notice changes in those closest to us. Perhaps your partner is wearing a new article of clothing, or looking at him or her reminds you about some new interest your beloved recently shared with you. By observing what's new about your partner, you strengthen your ability to see and engage with him or her in new ways.

Sometimes those little changes go unnoticed for a long time. We all get into routines in which we become blind to our partners' growth. Couples that grow apart do so because they fall out of communication with each other. Wabi Sabi Love brings us back into conversation with each other as it allows sufficient space for observing and telling the truth.

FIVE

The Yin and Yang of Deeper Love

Your task is not to seek for love, but merely to seek
and find all the barriers within yourself that you have
built against it.—*Rumi*

What gets in the way of deeper love? Take it from Rumi:
the barriers to that which we seek exist only within ourselves. If we want to be listened to, we have to learn to listen. If we want unconditional love, we first need to grant it
to others and ourselves. We can greatly influence our relationships just by changing the way we act toward others. To
paraphrase Gandhi, deeper love can only be found if we are
willing to be the change we want to see.

What does it take to truly listen to our beloveds? How can we hear without all the unconscious filters we've developed so we can tune in to our mates' realities and fully embrace what they think, feel, and believe? How can we move beyond ourselves to actually see the beauty within our partners?

In this chapter you will find the path to deeper intimacy, purpose, and passion by learning how to tune in to yourself and your partner through fully engaging in each other's reality. But before you can tune in to your partner's reality, you first have to learn how to tune in to yourself. Wabi Sabi Love requires a deep listening to one's own intentions and beliefs. Without an understanding and love of self, Wabi Sabi Love cannot emerge.

Our friends Vivian and Mike found themselves in a pivotal moment early on in their marriage. Their story beautifully illustrates how *feeling into one's partner's deepest desire* lays the foundation for greater intimacy, trust, and unexpected outcomes.

THE BLENDING OF YIN AND YANG

In the fall of 1999, on the sunny Greek island of Ios, Vivian, a high-powered Boston-based marketing consultant accustomed to making things happen, met Mike, a multitalented techie from Minneapolis who had recently produced a feature film. Both were attending an archeological journey through Greece led by a Jungian analyst. Mike was captivated by Vivian's beauty, intellect, career-oriented drive, and independence. She was impressed with his focus, his bawdy sense of mischief and humor, and seemingly endless supply of yinlike creativity. And most important—unlike other men she had dated—Mike didn't seem the least bit intimidated by Vivian's yanglike ambition, strength, and ability to succeed in the world.

Sparks ignited throughout the days and nights of their Aegean adventure, and they quickly became a couple with marriage on the horizon. Vivian, in her East Coast, no-nonsense way, was very direct with Mike right from the start about her desire to have a family. He was on the same page about having kids, but he waffled back and forth about the timing and thought they could wait five years.

In her typical yanglike way, Vivian replied for the hundredth time:

"No way. I'm thirty-eight. We can't wait."

A few months later, sitting in a parked car on a freezing cold night in Minnesota, they were once again discussing the baby issue. Vivian experienced a yinlike need like never before. It was as though her biological clock was ringing in every cell of her body. Overwhelmed by her soul's desire to nurture, she looked at Mike and said, "Can't you see that I must have something to care for?"

Her voice suddenly sounded strange, even to herself. It was as if someone, or something, was speaking through her. Bathed in her own feminine energy, she realized, as the words poured out of her, that it was her highest truth speaking.

"At that point what drove me craziest about the situation was my perception of his lack of empathy or compassion. I often thought, *Why can't he feel what I feel?*" He had always been so sensitive to her thoughts and feelings before this. It felt strange to depart from her can-do career-oriented self to a softer, more unfamiliar side.

Soon after, they married and agreed to start working on making a baby. And then Mike's travel schedule got really busy. Vivian, who now knew her ovulation cycle down to the hour, made sure they didn't miss the upcoming window of opportunity. The next time she was ovulating, she simply got on a plane and met Mike at his hotel in her native New York City, and, voilà, got pregnant with their son Zak.

The happy parents of one beautiful boy, they were ready and planning for baby number two. Vivian, now age forty, knew it wouldn't be easy, but she never imagined that within the year she would miscarry . . . twice. Despondent and depressed, Vivian could think of little else. Her desire for another child to nurture was as intense as her initial longing, and she began to seriously wonder how she would fulfill this overwhelming, driving need.

"And then one night, around three o'clock, I suddenly knew what I had to do. I woke Mike up and told him, 'I have to go to Africa. I must do something to help the children there.'"

Feeling the sincerity of her words, Mike simply said, "If that's what you need to do, go." He didn't question her, try to dissuade her, or warn her of the dangers.

The next day they drove to Los Angeles to attend a service at the Agape Church for the first time. As fate would have it, there was an announcement describing a special mission to Senegal and Gambia departing in three weeks' time.

Vivian's trip to Africa was life changing, as she became acutely aware of the needs of the children and mothers in these impoverished Third World countries. The statistics alone were heartbreaking: seventeen million people have already died of HIV/AIDS, resulting in some twelve million orphans. Each day three thousand children die needlessly from malaria.

As Vivian prepared for her return home, she suddenly recognized that her work in Africa would become her Wabi Sabi solution to her infertility—her way of discovering the inherent perfection in her inability to have a second child. She boarded the homeward-bound plane with an unwavering commitment to make a difference in Africa.

"Being a mother didn't just open my heart to my own child; it opened my heart to the needs of mothers and children around the world. My disappointment at not being able to have another child of my own opened me up to the possibility that all children were 'just like my child.' I knew that I had found my calling in Africa."

Thus, www.Justlikemychild.org was born. Within one month Vivian and a small team of supporters raised $30,000 to buy a generator that would supply electricity and water for a small hospital in rural Uganda that served more than 600,000 needy families. Within a few months they had enough money donated to hire a full-time medical doctor, buy an ambulance, and acquire much-needed supplies.

Mike's creativity fueled Vivian's mission as he designed new and unique fund-raisers to support the programs in Uganda that now include education for girls, building schools, a new surgical center, microenterprise, and malaria prevention, none of which would have been "birthed" had it not been for the couple's ability to listen to each other.

Years later Vivian reminded Mike of that cold night in the parked car when she revealed her desire to have children. She asked him, "What made you finally decide that you were okay with having a kid?"

What he said stunned her: "That night I heard your soul speaking to me, and I knew that I had to do this for you. I knew that the greatest gift I could give you was to help you fulfill your soul's desire and trust that this was right for us."

Agreeing to create a family was Mike's gift of compassion, his way of "feeling in" to his partner. This realization shattered Vivian's previous assumptions about Mike. For the first time she discovered that not only did Mike feel what she felt, but he trusted her enough to allow her soul's desires to guide them both. She saw that she had been so attached to her judgment that he wasn't compassionate and wasn't hearing her that she failed to see that all along the problem lay in her misperception.

Vivian and Mike's story is a powerful reminder that even when we think we know the content of someone's mind, we often don't. In other words, our partners may be "feeling in" to us more than we give them credit for. Psychologists and neuroscientists who specialize in cognition attribute this phenomenon to something they call the "Theory of

Other Minds." Simply stated, at a young age we develop the ability to recognize others as individuals and make inferences about what they are thinking or feeling. It's one of the most valuable cognitive tools we have with which to navigate our world of relationships.

According to neuroscientist Peggy La Cerra, Ph.D., "we maintain hundreds of memory records about each of the people we know—what they value, what motivates them and their particular likes and dislikes." In intimate relationships, this means that although many of us think we know what our partners are thinking at any given moment, it may not necessarily be true. They may be motivated by something completely different; but familiarity breeds a high level of comfort that can sometimes be assuming of the other person.

Most of the time, once the honeymoon phase has passed, we tend to pay attention to our partners only at the points of intersection between their behavior and whatever we're personally trying to accomplish in the moment. We move into autopilot and lose touch with our basic listening skills, assuming we know how the other person is feeling because "you've been down this road a hundred times before." As Vivian discovered, we often make the wrong assumption that our partners are unable to feel what we feel because each of us is living in a highly personalized internal world.

Often we don't even take the time to figure out what our partner is really thinking—or even saying.

For me, the practice of deeply listening held the key not only to attracting Brian into my life, but also to helping us get back in synch at a time when our relationship could have easily gone off the track.

Having grown up with the women's rights movement, I learned early on to place my nurturing side on the back shelf in the name of ambition and accomplishment.

On a positive note I grew up *knowing* that I was as smart (maybe smarter!) and as worthy as any man, despite my father's condescending comments about how he looked forward to seeing my sister and me "barefoot and pregnant" one day. Fortunately, Mom modeled the role of strong, independent businesswoman who could do anything, and I clung to that vision with all my heart.

The downside of my feminist "can do" attitude, however, is that my quest for independence and equality caused me to almost completely neglect my feminine side. I was so committed to my strong opinions about a woman's true role in the world that I identified almost entirely with my masculine side while allowing the feminine part of myself to wither. This became a major stumbling block for me as I later realized I could not tune in to love if I tuned out the most loving part of myself. My Wabi Sabi moment was the realization that I had to unearth my yin in order to magnetize my future yang partner.*

I am what you might call a bottom-line person, someone who speaks her mind and calls things as she sees them without any sugarcoating. In fact, no one would ever accuse me of being a wallflower! And while this masculine style of communication proved very useful in the workplace, I discovered it's not a quality most men find endearing or attractive in an intimate relationship. Masculine men tend to look for the feminine, yinlike quality in women, while feminine women tend to gravitate to the opposite, yanglike source. Apparently, my yang was in overdrive, and it wasn't until one fateful night that I realized how off-putting my yang-saturated self could be.

WABI SABI PRINCIPLE

When we are out of balance in our energies, our relationships become lopsided. Like two halves of a circle, each partner moves fluidly back and forth as in a dance. To avoid stepping on each other's toes, stay conscious of the energies to remain in step with your partner.

*According to Taoism, we all have a blend of both yin and yang. Yin is defined as feminine energy; yang is seen as masculine. We get into trouble in our love relationships when both partners become lopsided with too much of one kind of energy. A Wabi Sabi relationship provides a blend of both.

One evening when I was in my early thirties, I had been on a date with a man I found rather obnoxious, superficial, and patronizing. Okay, it was a really bad date. Completely unintentionally, this man we'll just call Dirk said something that changed my life: "You are one tough and powerful woman, and I'll bet you scare the shit out of most men."

After that comment, Dirk stopped the car in front of my apartment building and leaned over to kiss me goodnight. I dodged him, slipped out of the door, and ran for home, vowing never to see him again.

His final words to me, however, became an audio loop in my head, playing over and over again.

"You are one tough and powerful woman, and I'll bet you scare the shit out of most men."

Oy.

Until that moment I had never, ever thought of myself as being either tough or powerful. But the thought wouldn't leave my mind. What if Dirk was right? What if that was exactly how I was showing up and, therefore, I was the one chasing away potential love? Stunned, I was too embarrassed to discuss this new revelation with anyone.

A few weeks later a girlfriend invited me to a lecture by Dr. Pat Allen, a psychologist with a reputation for providing women with "strict dating rules" that would, if followed precisely, lead to commitment and marriage. That was the promise that first got me in the door of the auditorium near the UCLA campus in Westwood. What kept me coming back was Dr. Pat's wise and wonderful insights about "masculine and feminine energies." It turns out that my practical, assertive, and results-oriented approach to both work and play meant that my masculine, yang-drenched side had the upper hand, while my receptive, creative, and soft, feminine yin energies were dormant, hiding out in a corner of my heart I had yet to access.

Dr. Pat explained that men and women possess both masculine and feminine energies and that it is totally appropriate for a woman to tap into her masculine side while working. However, if she wants to be with a masculine man, she needs to learn how to access her feminine energy, because it's the polarity between the two that generates harmony and desire. Wow. Now I was beginning to understand what Dirk meant, but how in the world could I go from being me, the only me I knew, to some feminine version of me? Did I have to twist myself into a pretzel or bat my eyelashes and giggle to please men? Or was there an authentically feminine side of me hidden somewhere, like the unknown frontier, just dying to be discovered?

Intrigued, I decided to find out.

For the next several months Tuesday nights with Dr. Pat became my newfound religion as I began to wrap my mind and heart around allowing the woman in me to emerge. I have to admit it didn't come easily. I had grown so accustomed to my default position of taking control and making things happen that I simply didn't know how to turn that off at the end of the workday. Yet I also sensed that a big piece of my key to happiness was inextricably tied to developing the ability to surrender to the feminine energy that would more seamlessly complement a man's. More than anything, I knew I had to learn to love through my deeper, receptive, feminine divine self.

Searching for the next piece to my own personal puzzle, I took up belly dancing. What could possibly be more rooted in femininity and sensuality than that? Soon I was rolling my hips and shaking my booty with the best of them, but all the while I was still making demands and providing my unsolicited opinions to the men in my life. The path to my inner goddess seemed to be eluding me. Because I wasn't seriously involved with anyone at the time, my mission to transform the "tough and powerful Arielle who scared men" slowly faded into the background.

However, belly dancing had a more profound effect on me than I first realized. Moving my body in this way unleashed a seductive, feminine part of me that actually desired an audience. That revelation, coupled with applying to my love life some of the manifestation techniques that I had used to establish my successful business, placed me firmly upon the path to magnetizing the love of my life.

If you've read *The Soulmate Secret,* you know just how well those manifestation techniques worked! Soon after I started using them, I met Brian. We knew from Day One that we were destined to be together. Three weeks after we met, we were engaged and within a few months we were living together and began a new business partnership as literary agents.

Our new business relationship proved to be exciting but occasionally frustrating. Brian and I definitely had different work styles. Once I sit down at my desk, I make my list for the day and then stay highly focused on making things happen, preferably the sooner the better. I don't hang out at the water cooler, make small talk, or shop online. Brian, on the other hand, is a people person. He loves to chat and connect and make sure everyone in the office is doing okay. Regardless of how many projects are on his to-do list, he takes his time and carefully considers each one. He writes, then rewrites. He ponders, questions, and considers. After all that, when he's ready, he delivers something that is perfect. Generally, he delivers three days later than I would have. Today, I greatly admire, appreciate, and value his attention to quality and detail, but in the beginning it took a lot of getting used to, and admittedly there were days when I wished I could light a fire under him.

Over time, I came to accept the difference in our work styles, but there was still one thing that he used to do that made me absolutely crazy. He always wanted to talk shop during dinner. The wannabe goddess in me had finally figured out that in order to embrace, embody, and exude my feminine energy, I needed to drop my masculine persona at the end of the workday. I had created a soothing transition to summon this yang-to-yin transformation. After coming home from work, I would practice my belly dancing before soaking in a long, hot, aroma-infused bubble bath. Then I would put on a little makeup and a dress, and we would go out for dinner (for years we ate out nearly every night). But, inevitably, at some point between soup and dessert, Brian would begin discussing one of the books we were selling or a contract we were negotiating. Generally speaking, the conversation would go something like this:

BRIAN: I think the publisher's offer for John's next book will end up being close to $150,000, but they're asking for world rights.

ARIELLE: That's great! Can we talk about it tomorrow when we're in the office?

BRIAN: Why? We're here now, and this is fun!

ARIELLE: Yes, it is fun, but I really want to enjoy being with you tonight, and I don't want to put my brain into work mode.

Often, despite my best efforts to steer the conversation in a different direction, we would end up having what felt more like a business meeting than a romantic evening because it was easier than trying to explain something that I just couldn't quite describe in a way that Brian could understand. With each dinner conversation that turned to business, the knot in my stomach tightened and I prayed for guidance on how to explain to my new supercool jock husband that my inner goddess was starving for equal play time.

Then one day when I was looking through my bookshelf in search of a particular title, I came across a heavily marked-up copy of David Deida's *Intimate Communion*. As I flipped through the pages, I discovered once again how he elegantly explains non-gender-based masculine and feminine identities in a Western cultural context. Or in plain English: my situation exactly. Brian spent some time reading through the book, and we both agreed we would benefit from attending one of Deida's workshops.

So off we went to a retreat center in rural Oregon where we spent the weekend laughing, crying, eye-gazing, and dancing. Deida is intelligent, funny, profane, and at times downright obnoxious and arrogant. But despite some of his more blatant shortcomings, he's still a great teacher. From him, Brian and I discovered all the many reasons why we both needed to honor my emerging feminine energy by creating sacred space and boundaries to separate our working relationship from our intimate relationship.

We learned that in a healthy relationship each partner will express both masculine and feminine energies at various times and that for us, outside the workplace, Brian's preferred expression is masculine and mine is feminine. Brian realized that his desire to talk shop at dinner came from his years in the development business, spending long nights with his partners, hashing and rehashing the finer points of a deal. That was fun for him. But once he reaped the benefits of nurturing and encouraging my feminine expression, he became more than willing to forgo shop talk after hours. The Wabi Sabi moral of this story is that by really listening to each other, Brian and I discovered ways for each of us to express both our masculine and our feminine sides. And as a result, we became more compatible workmates and more passionate lovers.

Ultimately, our willingness to keep communicating our truth, our ongoing commitment to have our relationship be our number one priority, and our openness to trying new things resulted in a giant leap forward in our "intimate communion."

WABI SABI PRINCIPLE

When you feel into your partner's deepest desire, you create a foundation for more harmony, unity, and joy.

Once we began to deliberately direct the type of energy that flowed from whom and at what points throughout the day, the dance between yin and yang stopped being a tug-of-war and became something thoroughly enjoyable. For us, deepening our ability to listen to, hear, and "feel into" each other was the key to finding the right balance between our masculine and feminine energies.

Like two puzzle pieces in the yin-yang energy circle, Alanna and Mike are a couple that complement each other's strengths beautifully. In their story we discover that some Wabi Sabi lessons are learned in an instant, while others take eight months and thousands of miles to the ends of the earth.

THE 207-DAY SEARCH FOR THE SECRET
TO A HAPPY MARRIAGE

Once upon a time on a Sunday night, London-based Alanna was coerced into going to a pub on a blind date with a friend of a friend named Mike. Alanna assumed meeting at a pub was Mike's way of getting out of buying her dinner. Not expecting much from the rendezvous, she thought she would spice things up by fantasizing that Mike would be tall, dark, and handsome. When he arrived, a full five minutes late, she was disappointed to discover he was short with blond hair.

Her first words to him were "Where have you been?"

Mike's quick retort was "Really . . . that's how we start?"

But something quickly shifted, and within minutes they were laughing and talking as if they had known each other forever. Their first date lasted five hours. Three years later they were still going strong, enjoying a flourishing love for each other while living their lives with a sense of purpose and wild spontaneity.

With that in mind, one day Mike decided to participate in an extreme-sport event that required him to run seven marathons in seven days in the excruciatingly hot Sahara Desert. To stay connected to Mike and remind him how much he was cared for, Alanna created videos for him to watch every morning that included special messages from his family and friends.

"I began every day by crying while I watched these beautiful videos Alanna had made for me. By day three of the race my teammates who shared my tent finally asked me, 'Why haven't you proposed? She is amazing. She's a keeper, mate!'"

In what Mike describes as an "insight of biblical proportion" he decided they were right—it was time to propose. In between races he made a call to Alanna's father to set his plan into motion.

When his plane landed in London, Alanna, along with both of their families and many friends, were waiting to greet him. They all thought they had been invited to welcome home a tired but victorious Mike who had just run 151 miles in six days. Mike cleared customs and walked through the doors into the arrivals hall. The moment he laid eyes on Alanna, he got down on one knee and popped the question, with everyone watching, including many additional runners as well as hundreds of surprised travelers. Naturally, she replied with a resounding and heartfelt yes!

Before meeting Alanna, Mike had completed a motorcycle trip from New York to San Francisco and longed to do another big trip. Coinciding with this grand idea, Alanna and Mike had been discussing the rather disturbing statistic that half of all marriages end in divorce. They began to wonder about what makes one marriage successful while another fails. So, rather than plan a romantic honeymoon of sun, fun, and tropical drinks with paper umbrellas, they decided to take an amazing road trip to interview couples from Anchorage, Alaska, to the bottom of the Americas in Ushuaia, Argentina, to find the elusive answers to our collective marriage dilemmas in hopes of making an interesting and entertaining documentary film.

On June 21, 2009, they began their adventure in a Russian-built motorcycle with sidecar. Mike, Alanna, a video camera, tripod, assorted gear, clothing, and two laptops were all squashed into the pint-size vehicle, leaving them both feeling like sardines. But with a spirit and sense of excitement so big, their only thoughts were to put pedal to the metal into the unknown.

Over the next 207 long days and nights, they drove through 15 countries, conducted 120 on-camera interviews with couples of all ages and backgrounds, and eventually completed their journey on February 26, 2010.

During their three-year courtship they had come to know each other's habits and quirks, some of which they figured they would just have to put up with since neither seemed willing to change.

"Mike has a trait that his mother refers to as 'stickability' and that I call simply 'work Mike.' Ever since he was a small child, he has had the ability to focus so intently on something that once he puts his attention on it, nothing can deter him. In his world, literally nothing else exists," Alanna explains. "Mike's focus is to the total exclusion of everything else. When he is in that state, I just can't get through to him."

For instance, she will remind him, while he is in the middle of a home-improvement task, that they need to leave the house in twenty minutes for an appointment. She'll then give him a nudge ten minutes later. He will say okay, and then fifteen minutes later she finds him with a drill in one hand and a shelf in the other, expecting her to understand that "I just had to put this up."

Or she'd phone him at work, let him know what she was cooking for dinner, and ask him what time he would be home. Something at work would capture his attention, and two hours later he still wouldn't be home.

This obsessive behavior meant that they were always late for everything. It was the source of their biggest arguments and created real frustration for Alanna.

Mike's biggest complaint about Alanna was of a very different nature. His nickname for her is "chatty Lanny" because she is always talking, especially when he is trying to talk. Alanna has ADHD tendencies, a big contrast to Mike's Zen-like precision and ability to focus. She is not able to concentrate on anything for more than five minutes.

Before the start of their big trip, they knew they were going to be together 24/7 for eight straight months, and each secretly worried how they would survive the one thing that drove them crazy about the other. They quickly discovered something that completely amazed them.

On one of their first days in Alaska, "work Mike" was in full force. He had organized everything: the motorbike, camera, and all the other necessary ingredients. He had even studied all the equipment and learned everything about it. In addition to his equipment preparation, he was doing all the driving. Alanna felt useless, as if there were no reason for her to be there, which played directly into all her insecurities and sensitivities.

After a deep heart-to-heart discussion, they realized they needed to figure out a role for her. Since the success of the documentary and the trip required married couples to be interviewed, it became Alanna's job to find the interviewees. Within no time she was talking to everyone, calling agents to secure interviews with assorted authors and VIPs, striking up conversations with people in the streets, and even finding some fascinating people in restaurants and bars. In every town they drove through, she ultimately found all the couples that would be interviewed for the documentary. Mike enthusiastically discovered that his "chatty Lanny" possessed the incredible ability to talk with profound understanding to total strangers.

"We interviewed all sorts of people from all walks of life about very deep-seated emotional issues. We also asked extremely personal questions about their marriages, but with Alanna acting as the interviewer, she put them at total ease, bringing out deep information while I handled the camera and technical aspects of the interview."

Alanna saw that she could use the gift of "work Mike" to their advantage. They'd begin most days at nine o'clock, and "work Mike" would stay totally focused on driving and keeping them on track, often driving an astonishing ten hours a day.

"Funnily enough, this trip made me love 'work Mike' in a way that I could never have imagined. Now I know I have a man who, when he puts his mind to something, sees nothing else until he gets it done. Distraction is not part of his vocabulary. This meant he could fix the bike when it broke down and at the same time figure out how, as a novice filmmaker, to keep our equipment running. He could even write e-mails in Spanish."

Alanna now knows how to handle this characteristic and to use it to their greatest advantage. Most important, it's something she now absolutely loves about him.

"On the trip we were brilliant together. What an amazing gift he has to get things done with such dedication, while I'm such a flutter-headed distractible fool! Without wanting to get all sentimental, I think he's going to make a great father as a result! He'll learn to change nappies and do it like a pro. I bet he'll even build tree houses!"

Today when Alanna sees that Mike is in his own world and far from reality and she needs him, she has learned ways to slowly bring him back to planet Earth.

As for Mike, he admits that by the end of the trip, he clearly saw the value of "chatty Lanny."

"Alanna's ability and willingness to connect with people from all walks of life was incredibly important. We couldn't have done this without her amazing people skills. In the past I was always apologizing to my mates about her constant chatter. Not anymore," he says.

Today they are like yin and yang, finishing each other's sentences while Alanna writes a book about their amazing and wildly fun adventure and Mike edits the documentary and captures their exciting and once-in-a-lifetime journey.

Imagine a world in which we truly listened to each other like the couples in this chapter. Peggy La Cerra believes that we can develop the ability to become much better listeners and consciously develop a sense of the other's experience— to feel into them and expand our "theory of their mind." To do this, she offers the following exercise:

EXERCISE: *Visiting the Other's Reality*

Pick a time when the two of you will be alone together for two hours or more. It can be while you are having a meal, going for a walk, or just doing some mundane household chores.

For the first hour it will be your turn to visit your partner's reality. Whatever she is doing, her job is to tell you her perspective on whatever is happening for her in the moment. Your task is to listen intently in order to gain a deeper understanding of her experience. Essentially, as the observer, you are there to ask engaging questions so that you can more fully understand her from the center of *her* reality, rather than yours. This is a loving practice that is not about judgment or criticism, and at any time either of you can gently suggest another way in which you would like your partner to interact with you.

At the end of the first hour, switch roles and invite your partner to step into *your* reality.

With each practice, you'll deepen your ability to listen to and *feel into* each other.

Recognizing the uniqueness of each individual, learning to work with your yin and yang, and developing your "feel into" ability are essential Wabi Sabi skills to cultivate because they help us to show up and stay present for the times when we need to have the hard talks with our significant others, or they with us. Developing the ability to listen with all our senses deepens trust and makes it possible for both partners to communicate the good, the bad, and the ugly with love and compassion. The more adept we become at hearing both what is said and unsaid, the more we open the door for true intimacy.

SIX

It's Never Too Late

When the Japanese mend broken objects, they fill the cracks with gold. They believe that when something's suffered damage and has a history it becomes more beautiful.—*Barbara Bloom*

As we walk down the aisle in anticipation of our eternal union with our mates, we aren't thinking about what might happen should things go south between us or how we might cope if we discovered that our partners had been deceitful. Most of us allow our romantic ideals to take the lead and hope for a long-lasting monogamous relationship, like swans or a pair of prairie voles.

But none of us escapes being touched by divorce.

My parents divorced when I was sixteen. I was in the midst of my teenage rebellion years, and I don't recall being too involved or even affected by it. After all, I was pretty emotionally suppressed and checked out at the time. A lot of pot-smoking and other forms of debauchery account for my lack of insight into my emotional state when my parents split.

The next divorce I witnessed was absolutely heartbreaking. My sister, Debbie, had married a handsome Jewish Ivy League–educated doctor with whom she had a healthy adorable baby boy before their first anniversary. They moved into a beautiful home with an ocean view and frequently invited me to join them for dinner. I remember being impressed with their new (matching!) dinnerware and elegant Italian hand-blown glass oil and vinegar servers. It was equally impressive that he went to his office to see patients every day and spent a lot of nights and weekends reading charts and working hard to support his new young family. Debbie was busy around the clock with the baby and with shopping, cooking, and decorating their beautiful new home. From the crystal wineglasses to the shiny new car in the driveway, everything about their new life together seemed sparkling. Yet before their second anniversary could be celebrated, their marriage and seemingly happy existence were over. On paper they had been perfect for each other.

In reality, they were two different people with dreams and visions for their future that were totally incompatible.

I watched my sister become a flurry of emotions and almost paralyzed by her distress. One moment she was sad and despondent after crying for hours. The next moment she would become furious and full of rage. She was fearful, powerless, and, at moments, feeling very lost. Her dream of an idyllic family life, the one she always wanted, had been shattered in what seemed like the blink of an eye. The one thing that kept her going was her faith and determination to heal her heart. She maintained the courage to create the best life possible for herself and her son while demonstrating an unyielding commitment to healing herself. She truly wanted to find a way to befriend her ex-husband so that they could harmoniously coparent their son. In fact—true Wabi Sabi style—she translated the lessons learned during this grueling yet awakening process into the topic of her perennially bestselling book *Spiritual Divorce: Divorce as a Catalyst for an Extraordinary Life.*

WABI SABI PRINCIPLE

Even in the darkest, most dangerous moments of a marriage, healing is possible when truth is shared with sincerity and vulnerability.

As if surrounded by a house of cards, over the next few years I witnessed several other friends' whole existence crumble as they went through soul-shattering divorces; they, too, experienced varying degrees of anger, fear, heartache, helplessness, sadness, and grief. The level of pain they experienced didn't seem to change whether they were the dumper or the dumpee. Ever aware of the dreary statistics on divorce, I began to wonder whether a lifelong partnership is even possible. Could Wabi Sabi Love heal these wounds? Was it really the true answer to couples on the verge?

Searching for answers to my pressing questions, I made the most beautiful discovery. There actually *are* people who teeter on the brink of disaster but then find a renewed equilibrium that makes them stronger, more empowered and richer for it. The couples you are about to meet exhibit the fundamental shift that occurs in relationships when we move beyond a relationship built on lies to one built on truth. These people taught me that we all make mistakes. Sometimes they are small; sometimes they are seemingly insurmountable. But Wabi Sabi can help us honestly address and face every one.

These couples are living proof that when we learn to truly become Wabi Sabi artisans, light can indeed be found at the end of even the darkest tunnels.

THE HEART TO FORGIVE

Jean-Paul had been Mia's lover, best friend, and soulmate for nearly three decades. Together they raised three daughters. Because they were a very happily married couple, Mia fully expected their love to last forever.

In 1999 Jean-Paul had a heavy travel schedule for work in Venezuela. While Mia certainly missed him, his extended absence also made her aware that she had lost some of her passion for Jean-Paul and had begun to take him for granted. There was even a part of her that was hoping for something to happen that would spark an improvement in their relationship.

The moment Mia met Jean-Paul at the Dallas airport, she sensed something was wrong. There was a tightness in his jaw and an aloofness that made her feel uneasy. As they drove home, a frightening coldness slithered between them.

For the next few days, they said little to each other until Mia began to question him. "What's troubling you?" she asked. She repeated the question a few more times over the course of the week, and every time he gave the same response.

"Nothing."

But her intuition was strong. Deep inside her she knew something had occurred in Venezuela. She was determined to find out the truth.

Just when she felt as if her head were an eggshell about to crack, she turned to him in the kitchen one day and blurted it out: "Jean-Paul, I know something happened in Venezuela. I'd like to know two things: her name and what she looks like."

He sucked in some air, then leaned back on his heels. He surveyed the landscape of his wife's face for quite a while before finally speaking.

"What do you mean?" His eyelids quivered.

She drew a long breath before she continued. "You can tell me," she assured him. "Talk to me, *the friend,* not the wife."

He steadied himself as he took stock of what Mia had said. Should he tell her he had been having an affair with his secretary, Efelia, a thirty-four-year-old single mother of a young son who had led a tragic life? He summoned his courage and explained that their relationship had begun as a simple friendship, but in recent weeks it had evolved into much more.

Mia's heart sunk in anguish. While he emptied his soul, she stood stock still, not daring to utter a word. Jean-Paul went on to tell her about the tragedies of Efelia's life: her father had committed suicide; her boyfriend had died of a heart attack; another man had gotten her pregnant and gone off to marry someone else. Mia could see that Jean-Paul felt pity for her and that he was clearly confusing pity with love.

Shattered and crushed, Mia spent the next few days crying one moment, then raging the next. One day, in a fit of anger, she broke every plate and glass while emptying the dishwasher. Despite her internal wrath, she did her best to not let Jean-Paul see the extent of her pain. She wanted to fight to save the marriage, but at the same time she wanted Jean-Paul to be free to leave if that was what he really wanted. She told Jean-Paul he deserved to be happy and that if it was going to be with someone else, then she wouldn't stand in his way.

Jean-Paul stood at a major crossroads, facing a decision that would change his life forever. "Mia's compassionate response completely snapped me out of my stupor," Jean-Paul admits. "Deep in my heart I knew I wanted to be with her."

Work required that Jean-Paul return to Venezuela a few weeks later. Before he left, he promised Mia that he would no longer be physically intimate with Efelia. She wanted to believe him and prayed he would keep his promise. Still believing that the love she and Jean-Paul shared was "sacred," Mia decided to exercise patience despite her feelings of doubt.

As Jean-Paul sat at the gate at the airport, he strengthened his resolve. He had every intention of telling Efelia the affair was over the moment he landed in Venezuela. He even sent Mia an e-mail from the Dallas airport, telling her that he hated himself for causing her so much pain and assuring her that she was not responsible for his straying. Nothing was going to stop him from proving his love to Mia.

What happened next left Jean-Paul gasping for air. When he landed in Caracas, Efelia revealed to him that she was pregnant. Just hours after he promised his wife that everything was over with Efelia, he discovered that they would be tied together for life through the birth of a child. Efelia said she hadn't planned the pregnancy, and they both admitted they had been careless. Neither was willing to entertain the possibility of an abortion.

Jean-Paul was filled with dread. Just that morning he had received an e-mail from Mia telling him she would love him forever. Now he would have to break her heart once again with the news that he was about to become a father.

Mia's reaction to the news was as Jean-Paul anticipated. Her pain, anger, humiliation, and despair were excruciating. Conflicted between her desire to save the marriage and her fear that this baby would tie Jean-Paul and Efelia together forever while breaking them apart, Mia wrestled with feelings of loss and confusion.

Jean-Paul apologized profusely while professing his love for Mia and begging for her forgiveness. During this time he also shared with Mia that expecting another child at age fifty-three made him feel young again and that he intended to give the child his name and financial support.

Mia prayed she could find the strength to get through this nightmare. She tried to make peace with the situation while doing her best to shift her spiraling-downward moods into something more empowering. As a way to cope and also distract herself from the pain, Mia began to volunteer at a shelter for abused women. It was there that she saw how her pain paled in comparison to what the women in the halfway house had gone through. They had suffered losses far greater. Somewhere in the depths of her heart, she realized she had gained the very thing she had asked for during his long absences: the spark that would motivate her to renew her love for her husband. From the deepest part of her soul, she decided to completely forgive him.

One day while journaling, she wrote herself a daily prayer that served as a turning point in her healing process:

God, I ask you to use me.
Take my fears, my arrogance, my failures, my ignorance,
And use me to serve those on my path.
In sadness or in joy. In hatred or in love.
Use me, Lord. Use me in any way.

A few months before Efelia gave birth, Jean-Paul was transferred to Venezuela full-time. Mia agreed to move with him. As she thought about being physically close to her husband's ex-lover and soon-to-be-born baby daughter, a new level of fear arose within her. She knew this challenge would be one of the hardest she had ever faced, but she was determined to accept Jean-Paul's child and support his decision to include her as a part of their lives. Fortunately, Efelia's heart was in the right place; she even wrote Mia a letter in which she shared that Jean-Paul admitted how in love he was with his wife during the short time he and Efelia had been together. At the core of her being, Mia knew that her husband loved her, and this near-marriage-ending crisis inspired him to find new ways to continually and earnestly demonstrate his love to her. He also kept his word about ending his intimacy with Efelia.

When baby Sabrina was born, Mia told Jean-Paul that he could spend as much time with his daughter as he wished, realizing that his love for this child took nothing away from their deep love and connection for each other. In fact, on some level, the baby enriched their lives and strengthened the love that held them together. For the two years they lived in Caracas, Sabrina spent nearly every weekend with them. After they moved back to the States, she has come to visit her half-sisters in Texas, and although she speaks little English, they remain in close contact.

"This difficult and painful experience made me who I am today," says Mia. "Having the heart to forgive is the reason why Jean-Paul and I are still together. What we realized is that by my forgiving Jean-Paul, we both healed on a very deep level, and now we share a vibrant, passionate, and sacred love with each other that is stronger and more meaningful than we ever thought was possible."

WABI SABI PRINCIPLE

Forgiveness and sincere apologies for wrongdoing are the foundation of a healthy and lasting relationship.

When Mia first shared her story with me, I remember thinking, *This woman is unbelievably strong as well as courageous.* She allowed herself to feel and express the full force of the anger and sadness of the situation, while at the same time keeping her focus on what she knew to be true in her heart: she and Jean-Paul were meant to be together. With Wabi Sabi clarity, Mia was committed to doing whatever it took to become recommitted and reengaged in their marriage. Despite her fear, she rode out the storm of Jean-Paul's affair with an open heart and clear intention.

Mia learned that the only thing she can control is her response to circumstances. Life, much like the weather, is not something you can control.

WABI SABI PRINCIPLE

A Wabi Sabi artisan takes a bird's-eye view of the situation before choosing to react. A shift in position can change everything.

Moody weather patterns are something with which I am very familiar. After all, I spent my stormy youth in South Florida where tropical rainstorms, thundershowers, and even sun showers occur on a near-daily basis. Unless you're a meteorologist or a farmer equipped with an almanac and a marrow-deep knowledge of the land, the weather is almost impossible to predict.

I remember one day in particular. I was looking out the front window at the rivers of torrential rain streaming down the pane. The sky was filled with low-slung clouds so dark and gray that they appeared to be a mile thick. From my vantage point, I guessed that the rain would last for hours. I'd been planning to go for a nice long run on the golf course, but it looked as though the rain would hinder my intention. Instead, I figured I would kill some time by watching TV. As I walked into the family room at the opposite end of the house, I saw that it was filled with glimmering sunlight. Confused, I opened the back door. As I walked onto the patio, I was delighted to discover that it was clear and sunny in our backyard. How was it possible that in a space of less than fifty feet the weather could be so dramatically different? Within a few minutes the sun was shining on the front of the house as well.

I often think about that day when I am stuck in the doom and gloom of a situation that appears to be out of my control. My mind tries to convince me that the situation is a particular way and there is no way out. And yet when I shift my viewpoint, the entire landscape can change in an instant.

Wabi Sabi Love can not only rescue relationships from big, devastating mistakes; it can also breathe new life into relationships that have become dull and faded through time. As you will see in this next story, Susan was convinced that divorce was the only solution to her chilly, stormy, rainbowless marriage. But unexpectedly, a total change of scenery and a brand-new environment transformed her life forever.

REDISCOVERING LA DOLCE VITA

From nearly the first moment they met, Susan loved Tim's spirit. He was always joking around, and they shared a similar appreciation for sarcasm and wry humor. As students at the University of Dayton, they lived in the same apartment complex and slowly but surely they got to know each other on a casual basis. It was humor and shared values that magnetized them to each other, and after five years of dating, they married. Laughter was certainly the bond and the soundtrack of their early days together.

Tim worked in radio sales and management and was quickly making a big name for himself. With two young children in tow and Susan maintaining a career as a teacher, life became more complicated as Tim rose through the ranks to become a powerful and respected "radio guy." His work required them to move frequently, taking them to Atlanta, Charlotte, Washington, DC, and eventually Los Angeles.

"Not only were we continually moving to a new city, we often moved multiple times within each city," Susan recalls. "I remember thinking on more than one occasion, *'This is not what I signed up for!'*"

It was when they moved to Los Angeles that their marriage really began to implode. Without realizing it, they quickly became ensconced in the consumptive, upwardly mobile Southern California lifestyle.

Both Susan and Tim had grown up in modest homes founded on strong values and tight-knit communities. Yet they now found themselves surrounded by wealth in a highly materialistic environment. The intensity of daily life was creating new levels of stress for them. Tim had a grueling one-hour commute each way to work in heavy traffic, along with the pressures of competing in the number one radio market in the country. Susan was just as busy as a stay-at-home mom, working on her master's degree while staying fully immersed in the lives of the kids and driving them through the daily gridlock and suburban sprawl of L.A.

Over the next five years, most of the intimacy and connection that had once been so precious to them was lost. As their responsibilities increased, they grew further and further apart, and before they knew it, they had almost no connection or real understanding of each other.

Tim felt that Susan wasn't supportive of his demanding career, and Susan felt that Tim didn't appreciate the demands of running a home and attending to the daily needs of two young children. In spite of attempts at couple's therapy, things were only getting worse, and Susan began to experience what she describes as a deep "soul level" of unhappiness. With great sadness, she made an appointment with an attorney to begin the process of ending her eighteen-year marriage.

"We hit our emotional ground zero after a series of arguments and spectacular fights about who was working harder, who was ignoring the other person, who was the better parent, who was spending more money, and who just didn't care about being married anymore."

A few days after her secret visit to the attorney, Tim asked Susan to help him organize and attend an upcoming six-day business trip to the Italian Riviera, escorting forty of his radio clients through fancy hotels, fine food, and upscale sightseeing in Florence and Portofino. Playing devoted wife on a trip like this wasn't new to Susan, and she agreed, thinking that it would be her final appearance in the role of dutiful wife. (Besides, getting to see Italy for the first time had its own appeal.)

As Susan recounts in her book, *Halfway to Each Other: How a Year in Italy Brought Our Family Home*, Italy was love at first sight. Walking through the ancient, charming streets of Florence, surrounded by the beauty and magnificence of the basilicas and the art quite simply blew her heart wide open in a way that took her by surprise. After years of living beneath a cloak of desperation, she felt a shift taking place in her soul.

On the fourth day of the trip, Susan awoke at sunrise. They were staying in a small hotel along the coast in the town of Santa Margherita. Mesmerized by the gorgeous ocean view, the gentle sea breezes, and the captivating morning light as it played on the harbor, she felt strangely calm and decided to wake Tim up to enjoy the scenery with her.

They sat on their balcony with their coffee while drinking in the beauty of the surroundings when Tim quietly said out loud, "I could live here."

"Me, too."

"No, I really could live here."

And with those fateful words began a conversation of a new beginning as they seriously began to explore the possibility of living in Italy.

With only two days left in their Italian holiday, they came up with a detailed game plan. If they could find an American school nearby and if they could find a suitable fully furnished apartment, they would take it as a sign that they were meant to make this bold and yet potentially disastrous decision. Even with a loving and healthy marriage, relocating to another country would be considered a risky move.

By that afternoon, despite the fact that neither of them spoke Italian, they had found an International School, which just happened to have two openings, one for each of their children, fourteen-year-old Katie and ten-year-old Matt. The headmaster of the school referred them to a real estate agent who assured them he had the perfect rental for them.

"We walked into an expansive and aesthetically beautiful apartment that was open and bright with ocean views from every room. With three bedrooms, three bathrooms, and three terraces, it was more than I had even hoped for," remembered Susan.

Within the hour they had signed a one-year lease. Italy would be their new home!

When they returned to Los Angeles, Tim immediately resigned from his job. They sold their house and some of their belongings and put the rest in storage. Within two months they were living in the small town of Nervi near Portofino. Their friends wondered if they had lost their minds.

The adventure came with many ups and downs. Surrounded by people who only spoke Italian in a culture completely foreign to them, everyday tasks—from grocery shopping to riding a bus—became major puzzles that needed to be solved. The amenities of the good life they had grown so used to—having a car, grocery stores filled with their favorite prepackaged foods, watching cable TV with five hundred channels—were quickly replaced with long walks, board games, and new adventures in eating. Most important, they began to learn to work closely and effectively as a team.

"We had to talk to each other because no one around us spoke English. Daily life became funny, scary, painful, and exhilarating. We didn't know what we were doing . . . and every day brought another seemingly insurmountable task."

One week into the move Susan experienced a moment of grace while listening to opera on the radio as she mopped the floors.

"I was gazing out the window, looking over the red tile roofs, the churches, and the ocean in the distance and felt overwhelmed by the sense of beauty and grace of the moment. I closed my eyes and said a prayer. I thanked God for our many blessings, for leading us to this threshold of opportunity, and then giving us the courage to embrace it. I had made peace with the fact that Tim and I felt unfulfilled and inept at our marriage situation. I did not want to live in the mire of negativity and blame any more. I had, instead, chosen to embrace hope with the knowledge that we were trying to do something about it. I felt we were poised on the edge of a year filled with finer moments."

One morning, six months into their adventure, Tim announced that he wanted to show Susan a new town he had discovered. They got the kids off to school and then jumped on the train and headed to Camogli.

"When we arrived, we walked down the steps to the coast. Spread out before us was this stunning multicolored fishing village. We wandered the streets until we found the perfect little café to hang out at and people-watch. As we were sitting and drinking our cappuccinos, I was overcome by a sense of great peace and realized that in an unspoken way we had forgiven each other for not being perfect. We had rediscovered the euphoria and deep connection that we shared in our earlier days. I now knew that a miracle had taken place. We were, quite simply, happy together, and I felt for the first time in a long time that everything between us was going to be okay."

At the end of the year they decided to return home. Although they had no idea where they were going to live, no jobs waiting for them, and new schools to find for the kids, Susan felt absolutely no fear.

"While the future was unknown, we were bonded as a family and nothing else really mattered. We were now four people who knew that in order to get the job done, we had to work together and, more important, share life's good fortunes with the ones we love."

Today, six years later they are happily living in Scottsdale, Arizona, with their family intact. Tim fulfilled a dream of starting his own company, and Susan is teaching at a local elementary school and doing freelance writing.

"In Italy we learned to accept each other for who we are without all the material things that had surrounded us in Los Angeles. We found out that we complete each other in a lot of ways. We learned that living together creates inherent friction, and we also came to see our friction as energy, not necessarily a problem. I learned that relationships are about transformation and renewal. They are about allowing each other the oxygen to breathe, the sunshine to grow, and even the rain to nourish the soil."

Italy exudes Wabi Sabi . . . the old, weathered buildings with faded facades that become more beautiful with each decade as the paint cracks and peels. Moving to Italy allowed Tim and Susan the time and space to rediscover themselves as individuals, as a couple, and as a family. By eliminating their former life of constantly acquiring more and newer shiny things, they adapted to Italy's more languid, sensual way of life, and in the process, love blossomed.

Tim and Susan's unusual rescue of their dying marriage proves to me that grace truly does exist when you trust your intuition. Susan trusted her inner knowing when she agreed to support Tim with his business trip, and they both trusted their gut instincts when they made the momentous decision to risk everything for a new life in Italy. Wabi Sabi is about embracing uncertainty and being willing to stand faithfully in those moments when you don't have it all figured out.

WABI SABI PRINCIPLE

Turn on the faucet of your intuition. When you listen with your heart, you see with it too.

But, what happens when your inner knowing sends you seemingly conflicting messages? The next story, which may be challenging for some of you to read, offers an important perspective on Wabi Sabi Love, one that entails discernment, responsibility, and ultimately forgiveness and compassion.

LIES, BETRAYAL, AND THE
REDISCOVERY OF BLISS

As a successful therapist, rock bottom was a place Jay had seen some of his patients reach. It was a place that he knew was essential for a person to reach to truly begin the emotional healing process. It just wasn't a place he ever expected to find himself in. For Jay, his rock bottom came as he stood in the tiny bathroom of his postdivorce Tulsa apartment and stared into his own eyes in the mirror. What he saw he didn't like at all: it was as if he were staring at a complete stranger.

Deep down he knew he was 100 percent responsible for creating the events that led to his *dark night of the soul.*

In 1997 a mutual friend introduced Jay to his wife, Julie, a stunning former beauty queen and model. Sparks ignited from the moment they met, and after a brief courtship they married in a simple ceremony in Eureka Springs, Arkansas. The loving couple was surrounded by close friends and family, including Jay's son from his first marriage. They began their life together with the belief that theirs would be *a marriage made in heaven, a marriage to last a lifetime.*

They focused on buying a new home, getting pregnant, and spending time with Jay's young son. Within eighteen months of the wedding, they had a baby daughter to add to their joy. Two years later a second baby girl arrived with the same fanfare.

For Jay, nurturing his new family, building his business as a therapist, working days in a children's hospital, and seeing private patients at all hours of the night became his obsession. Within a year he was seeing forty to fifty people a week, working twelve-hour days, and gaining a reputation for getting results with clients who presented extremely difficult cases.

"I wanted to make sure that Julie had all the gadgets she needed to be successful in her new role as a mother. I willingly deferred meeting any of my own needs so that my family was well provided for. And, of course, I hoped all of this would bring me the love and approval I craved."

However, from Julie's point of view, Jay poured everything into his work not for the sole benefit of his family but for his deep-seated desire to be rich and famous.

"I'd learned enough of his psychology jargon to wonder if he was a benevolent narcissist who was filling his own insatiable black hole for validation. In simple terms, I wondered if he was a jerk."

As Jay began to feel judged, criticized, unappreciated, and rejected, he deemed Julie an overly needy, demanding drama queen. Julie felt like a single parent who had to put up with a spoiled, manipulative, disrespectful stepson and a life that didn't meet any of her emotional needs. In spite of all this emotional turmoil, Julie's love for Jay never wavered.

Within just a few years, anger had almost entirely replaced passion. All trust had vanished. Yet, even as their foundation crumbled beneath them, they had a third child. This time it was a son.

"At this point," Jay recalled, "all we had left between us were bills, responsibilities, and our children. My only goal was merely to survive my marriage. I had no intention to really invest in it any longer."

While life at home continued to disintegrate, Jay became hugely successful as a consultant and executive coach. He often traveled for business and made time for excursions into the fantasy world of strip clubs and porn.

One very late night during a trip to Miami, Jay visited his favorite gentleman's club where he met a seductive young woman who wore black leather, spike heels, and red lipstick. She sauntered over to him and introduced herself as Dayanara. He quickly fell in love with her.

Jay convinced himself that at age twenty-six, Dayanara was mature and "well-integrated" because she had successfully extricated herself from an abusive relationship. After all, he reasoned, she worked in her own business by day and strip clubs at night to pay off her credit card bills. In spite of his extensive training as a psychologist, he still chose to play the role of white knight to the rescue.

"I wanted everything Dayanara represented: eroticism, freedom, vitality, and possibility. For the first time in years I felt alive."

In time, Dayanara quit her job as an escort to fulfill a role created especially for her in Jay's business. He believed that he could blend romance with making money and have a legitimate alibi to travel the country with her. He convinced himself that if he continued to provide well for his family, no one would get hurt, no one had to know, and everyone would benefit. But he was wrong.

Julie sensed something wasn't right and resorted to keeping track of Jay as much as possible. At one point she checked his e-mail and confronted him about the many, many e-mails she found from Dayanara. Jay did his best to convince Julie that Dayanara was simply an employee helping him to grow the business, but Julie continued to feel "a deep chill of unease and mistrust."

"I wasn't about to tell her the truth. I viewed our lives as a type of social quid pro quo. She got to be the upscale stay-at-home mom, live in a big house, and drive a new SUV.

"I got to provide it all and do whatever the hell I wanted to do. From my point of view, it was a fair deal."

As Julie's suspicions grew, she continued to search through Jay's desk and papers looking for evidence of an affair. She learned that he was using their personal money for a business Dayanara was starting, and she also discovered a signed lease for an apartment. She found e-mails and text messages, and she even hid a tape recorder in his car. He denied everything at first, then finally resorted to moving out to avoid Julie's hostility. Shortly after Jay's move, Julie was diagnosed with lymphoma.

The only thought that raced through her mind was what would happen to her kids if she were to die. She knew they might end up being parented by Dayanara. In that instant, it was clear to her that she would try the most aggressive treatment possible. The doctor warned her that it would leave her sick, weak, and in bed for long periods of time.

In an act of sheer will, Julie decided not to tell Jay the full extent of her illness. She didn't want his pity. She merely wanted his love and what was best for the children. In fact, she managed to arrange most of her chemo appointments so that their children would have one healthy parent around while she recuperated from the treatments.

Lost in his own needs, Jay just assumed Julie was trying to control him and thought she was lying about the seriousness of her illness. She wouldn't allow him to have access to her medical records. Slowly, Jay and Julie both came to the realization that their marriage was over. Jay didn't want to fix his marriage, and Julie saw he was not about to end his affair, so they agreed to begin the divorce process. His business with Dayanara continued to flourish. Soon Jay began looking to buy a home for the two of them in Miami.

For the next several months, things went from bad to worse. The kids were crying all the time, and Julie was still going through chemo. Not only was Jay constantly fighting with Julie, but his relationship with Dayanara was also starting to unravel. The illusion that he could have a real relationship with this seductress from the strip club was fading. He began to see her for what she was:

"She was the walking wounded. I began to see her as someone who lived every day in desperate need of constant adoration and sacrificial attentiveness from the man in her life."

Even though Julie still loved Jay, she had made a conscious decision to move on with her life. Julie began making plans to move herself and the children to Dallas to be closer to her brother. She explained to Jay that since he was only seeing the children twice a month anyway, moving to Texas wouldn't be a big deal and would actually create a higher-quality and less expensive life for her and the kids.

In that moment, Julie took a stand for her own life. She successfully completed her chemotherapy treatment and was ready to move forward without Jay. He was overwhelmed by her fortitude.

It was shortly after Julie's move to Dallas that Jay found himself looking into that bathroom mirror. Recalling all the events that had landed him there shook Jay to the core. His hair was drenched in sweat as he leaned into the mirror again to ask himself, *What if I have been completely wrong about everything? Did I really need to implode and devastate my family to experience the freedom and happiness I thought I deserved?*

One thing was clear: he had to end his relationship with Dayanara. The process was neither simple nor fast, but he finally cut ties with her for good. Even as Jay was beginning to find renewed interest in Julie, they finalized their divorce.

During this very uncertain time and determined to heal his issues, Jay began a serious inquiry into his own behavior and psyche. As a child, Jay had longed for love but had grown up in a volatile, alcoholic home surrounded by emotional abuse, poverty, and domestic violence, and as a result, he learned to both fear and avoid true intimacy. He saw that his choice to become a psychologist was a desperate attempt to rescue himself by becoming a savior to others: a creative compensation for deep-seated feelings of inadequacy.

Jay understood that it was time to break the entrenched patterns of his past and evolve and mature as a man. With this spark of clarity, he realized that Julie had always loved him in spite of himself. "I just didn't know how to receive her love, because I didn't know what love was."

He committed to spend more and more time with Julie and the kids. After declaring his intention to be the best friend and coparent possible, they even went on a family trip to Disney World the month after the divorce was finalized. The seeds of a possible healing were planted as they cautiously moved closer together. Despite all the chaos that had encircled them for so long, Julie never stopped loving Jay. She knew in her heart of hearts that the Jay who had acted out was not the person she knew him to be. Deep down she knew his behavior was not permanent.

A month after their wonderful visit to the Magic Kingdom, Jay found himself eating dinner alone at Rick's Café, a place where he and Julie used to eat often. As he sat near the crackling fireplace, waiting for his dinner to be served, he was filled with nostalgia. Feeling immensely sentimental and divinely guided, he opened his laptop and typed in the location of their wedding: Thorncrown Chapel in Eureka Springs. As he gazed at the images, he was transported back in time, recalling their ceremony and honeymoon ten years earlier. Then, with an almost otherworldly sensation, he began to see his future pass before his eyes like a movie on fast-forward. He saw unsettling picture frames filled with forced visits and divided holidays, unending resentments from the kids, awkward graduations, and all kinds of ugliness because he had abandoned his family. Jay knew in that moment, in every cell of his being, that he wanted to heal his past wrongs and pursue the possibility of a second chance. He was committed to making sure this movie would have a happy ending.

On an impulse, he made reservations at the cottage where they'd spent their honeymoon and convinced Julie to join him for a weekend devoted to exploring the possibility of building on the friendship they had created around the care of their children. As each day passed, Julie's trust and faith in Jay was rebuilt. She also saw areas in which she could grow to be the partner she wanted to be. They talked endlessly as they walked the streets of the quaint village, holding hands, hugging, and laughing as they reminisced about joyous events from the past. They became acutely aware of how they had each changed. In a moment of pure heart vulnerability, Jay won Julie back when he looked into her eyes and said, "My name is Jay. I'm interested in knowing who you really are, not what I've made up about you. I'd also like to tell you about who I am now, and who I want to become."

Those few words ushered in a new future, one dedicated to healing and the possibility of remarrying. Jay and Julie began the long road to recovery, filled with individual and couples therapy. During this time Jay experienced deep bouts of shame, berating himself for cheating on his wife and demolishing his family. One evening, as Jay was pouring his heart out to Julie, who held him as he sobbed tears of remorse, they heard the television in the background.

Looking at the screen, they watched in shock as New York governor Eliot Spitzer acknowledged his affair with an escort and apologized to his wife, family, and constituents. Jay was haunted by the look of pain and despair on Mrs. Spitzer's face. He had seen that same look on Julie's.

In a very solemn gesture, Jay sat down next to Julie, took her hand, and said, "Someone must tell the truth about infidelity: someone who will tell the absolute truth no matter the consequences. Affairs need deception in order to exist. To squelch infidelity, we must tell the transparent truth and nothing less. Maybe the terrible mistakes I've made can be redeemed if I can help others."

Even though it was Jay who had the affair, they acknowledged that they had both made mistakes in taking each other for granted and letting their connection wane. Eventually, Jay forgave himself, they forgave each other, and they remarried with a renewed sense of purpose and an entirely new definition of what a loving union means.

"True love requires us to evolve beyond our wounds, not demand that our partners or the relationship heal us from them," Jay says. "A great marriage is a product of design brought to life by new choices. To love another asks us to grow up, rise above how life has wounded us, and be responsible for what we need as adults."

WABI SABI PRINCIPLE

Wabi Sabi Love says you can evolve beyond your wounds to regain wholeness and grow a deeper and stronger love.

When I first heard this story, my reaction was one of disgust at Jay's actions. I couldn't imagine how or why Julie would be willing to stay with him. For several weeks I considered not including this story in the book because I felt that finding any beauty or perfection in Jay's actions was just "too big of a stretch." And yet I soon discovered the story's deeper truth.

One night Brian and I were in New York City for the book launch of *The Shadow Effect*, which was coauthored by my sister, Debbie Ford, Deepak Chopra, and Marianne Williamson. Each of them was taking a turn speaking about "the shadow" also known as our dark side—the negative emotions and behaviors we try to hide from ourselves and the world—such as our anger, greed, dishonesty, lust, jealousy, selfishness, and so much more.

To illustrate how easy it is to reject and repress one's shadow side, Marianne offered the following example: When a young child falls down and scrapes his knee and comes running to you in tears, you, the adult, take him into your arms and soothe him with kind words, kisses, and colorful bandages. However, when an adult is acting badly, in any of a million possible ways, it's much harder to extend this same comfort. In fact, we often shun and judge the person without realizing that his or her actions have been triggered by an internal wound that we cannot see.

Listening to Marianne speak on the stage that night, I had a lightbulb moment.

Even though I knew that Jay's actions stemmed from an abusive childhood, my reaction had been to judge him as undeserving of re-creating a loving life with Julie. But by continuing to love Jay and hold a possibility for a future with him—while simultaneously divorcing him and rightly protecting herself from his hurtful behavior—Julie helped him to make peace with the very shadows that had caused him to stray. This was an act of immense wisdom and courage. Her Wabi Sabi approach was to continuously hold the space for Jay to grow into the man she knew he was capable of being and to love him even when he was unable to love himself. For me, their story demonstrates that overcoming and healing from love's biggest obstacles is truly possible.

Julie and Jay are a testimony that love is possible not only in the presence of that which is whole, but in the presence of cracks and fissures, as well. Today they are committed to teaching other couples how to repair their marriages by filling in the cracks with healing acceptance, love, and forgiveness. Their story illustrates that we can learn from even the gravest of mistakes to become the Wabi Sabi artisans we are meant to be.

EXERCISE: *Writing a New Relationship Vow*

If you or your partner has broken your wedding vows, you may want to consider writing a relationship vow that describes your renewed commitment to the partnership. Think of it like a mission statement for your relationship that serves as a compass to guide your future actions and a testament to your commitment to move toward a shared future. A relationship vow is meant to be a springboard into your new reality as it proclaims your intention to be greater together than apart.

This exercise allows for a more inspiring future, the very thing that becomes the passionate everyday reality of a Wabi Sabi couple.

Here is one possible relationship vow you can tweak to fit your situation. Fill in the blanks below:

"For the past _____ years we have stood together through sorrow and joy, triumph and defeat, sickness and health, and together we have grown so much. We have evolved and transformed together. We have endured together, laughed and cried together. [*optional*: We raised a beautiful family together.]

I _____ take you _____ to be my _____ in cocreating a healthy, loving, supportive relationship as we recommit to a life together as best friends, lovers, and partners. On this day I joyfully promise to wipe away your tears with my laughter and soothe your pain with my caring and compassion. I will be the wind beneath your wings as we harmonize with a greater understanding of each other. We will heal the misdeeds of the past and renew our life together with honesty and transparency. I give myself to you completely, and I promise to love you always, from this day forth.

I promise to love and cherish you, respect you, and grow with you for all the days of our lives.

This is my solemn vow."

Wabi Sabi Love is based on the ability to be honest with oneself and the ability to be honest with one's partner. It is the willingness to share your truth, your whole truth, as soon as you know it.

EXERCISE: *Truth-Telling*

Relationships built on truth stand the test of time; those built on lies are guaranteed to go asunder.

No one knows this better than Barbara "Willow" Potter Drinkwater, a powerhouse entrepreneur from central Virginia who has dealt with her share of unreliable, deceitful partners. Life taught her that truth was the only way to make a relationship last. Now in a committed loving marriage, Willow has a great way of sharing her truth, even when she is frightened to do so. Leaning on Dwight Gold-Winde's teachings, she calls this process a RAFT, something she is **R**eluctant **A**nd **F**rightened **T**o Share. She starts out by saying "I have a RAFT." For those who know her, they are prepared. For those who don't, she explains that what she is about to say makes her uncomfortable but that she values the relationship so much that she is willing to step beyond her comfort zone to speak her truth. Then she says whatever she has to say in a few thoughtful sentences. It helps to be concise. As anyone who has had to endure a long-winded explanation will tell you, it typically turns into a shouting match or, worse, the speaker is often left ignored as the listener tunes out.

In this truth-telling exercise, I have provided some mini scripts for you to use when riding the RAFT on the river toward truth.

Perhaps your partner has just said something that hurt your feelings or that you interpreted as judgmental or critical. Find a quiet moment when neither of you is distracted or rushing out the door, then gently say:

"I honor you and our relationship. I have a RAFT I'd like to share."

Invite your partner to hop aboard as you paddle together down the stream of your imagination. Speak your truth in a few words using "I" statements.

I felt criticized when . . .

I am unhappy that . . .

I would like you to know that . . .

Conclude the conversation by thanking your partner for listening. Then ask whether he or she has a RAFT to share with you. Listen to what your partner says. Seal the discussion with a twenty-second hug. As Gay and Katie Hendricks rightly suggest, a twenty-second hug can heal a lot more than a bruised ego. It can solidify your truth-based relationship and bring your awareness for each other to a whole new level.

Hearing your partner's truth may not always be comfortable, especially when his or her behavior annoys you beyond measure. In those moments, applying the Wabi Sabi principle of acceptance can help immeasurably.

(If the truth-telling exercise feels a bit scary or intimidating, please download the guided process at www.wabisabilove .com/audio for a gentle introduction.)

SEVEN

Intimacy as Into Me See

Practicing love often means feeling through fear: intentionally opening yourself when you would rather close down, giving yourself when you would rather hide. Love means recognizing yourself as the open fullness of this moment regardless of its contents— trenchant thoughts, enchanting pleasures, heavy emotions, or gnawing pains—and surrendering all hold on the familiar act you call "me."—*David Deida*

When I was younger, I thought the word *intimacy* was a polite word for sex . . . as in "we had intimate relations last night" or "the date went great, especially when it got intimate." I was clueless. The worst part was, I didn't even know I was clueless. I had the world divided into two groups of people: those who I felt a connection with, and everyone else. For me, having a connection meant that some level of friendship had been established and I could be myself with that person. Somehow I wasn't quite willing to go to the deeper level of connection and friendship known as intimacy.

Intimacy, along with its cousin vulnerability, was something I avoided at all costs in my earlier relationships. I had perfected the art of skimboarding the shoreline of my emotional entanglements and had become a master of the light, breezy, and nonthreatening connection. In spite of my curiosity and interest in personal growth and all things spiritual, I managed to hang out in this deluded state of mind for a long time, dating men who were equally careful to avoid the potentially turbulent sea of vulnerability and intimacy.

One early morning sometime around 1993 I received a phone call from Kenny Loggins (yes, the famous singer/songwriter who penned, among many other titles, the theme songs for *Caddyshack, Footloose,* and *Top Gun*). We had a mutual friend who had suggested that I might be the perfect person to help find a publisher for a book project he was working on. The book was titled *The Face of Love,* a coffee-table book of images of couples making love, with the focus being on the expressions on their faces and the way they gazed into each other's eyes. With photography by Carl Studna, Kenny planned to write the text for the book, illuminating the art and practice of tantra. Tantra, he quickly explained to me, was a form of yoga, or sex as a spiritual path.

My ears perked.

For many years I had viewed sex as something of an adventure that both was fun and had the added benefit of being heart healthy (as in burning calories in an aerobic state), but not necessarily heart opening. Now, one of my favorite rock stars was telling me that sex could be fun, pleasurable, aerobic, *and* spiritual. He clearly had my attention. A meeting was arranged for me to meet with Kenny and Carl and review the photographs that had been shot for the book. I was captivated by the pure love and energy the couples expressed through their eyes and was certain I could find a publisher who would jump at the opportunity to bring this work of art to the world. Unfortunately, every publisher we pursued turned us down, but the experience opened my eyes and whetted my appetite to learn more about the connection of love, sex, spirituality, and intimacy.

Intimacy is not just about sexual relations, but about a deeper intersection between two souls. When we are truly intimate with another, we are free to completely be our most authentic selves. We feel seen, heard, and understood, and when we look into the other's eyes, there is the feeling of being "home." We can transparently share our innermost thoughts and fears as well as hopes, dreams, and aspirations. This level of intimacy is what I call a soulmate connection, and it can occur beyond just a romantic relationship. A soulmate can be your best friend, business partner, coworker, child, sibling, parent, or even pet. I believe we all have many soulmates in our lives. When we take the time to love, appreciate, and nurture these relationships, life becomes much juicier.

When I came across this next story about Wendy and Frank, I knew I had to share it because even though some of it may move you outside your comfort zone, the care, compassion, and tenderness that Wendy expressed toward Frank's issues provides a beautiful example of Wabi Sabi Love at its finest.

THE PATIENT LOVER

Wendy knew what it was like to be worshipped. A beautiful, petite actress, she attracted the type of men most women fantasize about. While in her early twenties, she had a wide spectrum of sexual experiences including relationships with famous narcissistic and overindulgent actors. She became consort to a well-known Tantra teacher and also dated a Qigong master who specialized in sexuality as a spiritual path.

As a teenager, her best friend had been murdered by a man who was obsessed with her. Because of that and other experiences, Wendy had begun to associate love and sex with danger and threat, which for a time was exciting but left her soul empty. It was during this period that she met Frank who would soon become her best friend and confidant. Frank didn't fit any of her delights and fantasies for romance. Wendy imagined herself with her version of tall, dark, and handsome. Frank's long blond hair, tie-dyed tank top, and flip-flops were a far cry from the sophisticated men she was used to. And yet, their instantaneous spark of love for each other seemed so pure and innocent . . . almost as if they could be twins. Wendy continued her sexual escapades and shared the details with her new best friend, Frank.

Frank had no problem listening to Wendy's sexual adventures. They were best friends, shared everything, and knew it was all about growth. He did, however, at times try to imagine himself in the role of one of the lovers she was describing and wished he could take one's place.

Eventually Frank moved to Atlanta, while Wendy remained in New York. Nearly every night they spent hours on the phone, bonding over their shared passion for finding a way to serve the world.

While Wendy was exploring the width and breath of sexuality, Frank was entering a ten-year period of celibacy. His first memories about sex came from his mother's stories about how dirty and dangerous sex is. When she was seventeen, she engaged in a heavy-petting session with one of many boyfriends. Even though there was no penetration, she managed to get pregnant (and for those who find this unbelievable, this is really what happened). She and the man who later became Frank's father decided to marry and have the baby. Four years later Frank was born. He grew up in an unhappy household, listening to his mother complain about her unfulfilling sex life. He grew up watching his mother have a nineteen-year affair with a neighborhood friend while observing his father become fatter and more passive with each passing year.

While in college Frank had a few girlfriends, but when it came to sex, he would always hear a voice in his head that reminded him that if he ejaculated in or near a woman, his life would be ruined. He even began to question his own sexuality. By the time he was twenty, he managed to have a few good, fulfilling sexual experiences with his girlfriend, but the relationship only lasted eighteen months, leaving Frank unfulfilled and confused.

At the young age of twenty-one he met Wendy. His fear of sexuality, and the fact that he had always imagined himself with a brunette rather than a blonde, was the perfect elixir to keep his relationship with Wendy platonic. Between daily phone calls and in-person visits nearly every month, they discovered they could share anything with each other on a fairly intimate and playful basis. Five years into their friendship they had their first kiss, which left Wendy breathless; without hesitation she told Frank, "You are going to make the most wonderful lover."

Rather than soak up the compliment, Frank's face turned white and his expression somber. The immediate and fearful thought of not being able to perform for Wendy made him shake in his boots.

So, for the next five years they became best friends with cuddle benefits (only). During this time, as Frank's confidence increased, he was able to see that Wendy really did love him unconditionally. He realized she was drawn to him for who he was at the deepest soul level.

During their eleventh year together as friends, they became very intimate and would sometimes come close to making love when suddenly all of Frank's fears would emerge. Soon he would tremble and shake from head to toe. Wendy would hold him, stroke his hair, and remind him that she was content even if they didn't make love. She would breathe with him and gently ask him questions to help him through the process of releasing his pain from past conditioning. Eventually Frank began to feel at ease. One day, with great tenderness and devotion, they consummated their relationship.

"My fears didn't suddenly disappear," Frank recalled, "but I began to realize that what I needed to do in this situation was not focus on my fear and doubt but rather ask myself, what can I do in this moment to give Wendy more love?"

Frank began to use a variety of stress-reducing processes to calm and prepare himself for Wendy's visits. He began to make the anticipation fun and reminded himself that his body, as well as his heart, could give her love. And even though their nights together often didn't always go as planned, the morning sun brought forth renewed passion. They discovered that Frank's fear would disappear with the darkness, and they would spend their mornings making love.

Their shared commitment allowed their sex life to unfold without an agenda and to be the highest expression of love in the moment.

Wendy's commitment to Frank and her ability to stay present with him allowed Frank to be extremely vulnerable and actually released him from his performance anxiety, which allowed their love to flow more freely and with much more passion.

"With Frank, my goal was never to have a great sex life, but to experience deep unconditional love and acceptance. The irony is that ultimately all of his old fears and perceptions cleared. Today we have a more wonderful, active, and exquisite sex life than any of my previous encounters with 'experienced professionals,' because the foundation of what we have is truly unconditional love and connection rather than performance."

Like Wendy, I had often mistaken sex for connection. Before Brian and I met, I frequently had the thought that *someday, when I am married, I am going to have sex nearly every day.* When we first got together, Brian was traveling constantly for business and we lived in different cities, so daily sex wasn't an option. When we began to live together, I discovered he was an early bird who was often out of bed by 5:00 A.M. (I was rarely awake before 8:00 A.M.) and sometimes asleep by 9 P.M. (midnight was my usual bedtime). We soon discovered that weekend afternoons were our ideal time for making love, which made daily sex impractical and nearly impossible. And while I had spent a lot of my earlier years fantasizing about daily sex, a remarkable thing happened. I realized that what I had been seeking and yearning for all along was something that I now had . . . a deep, loving, intimate soul connection with someone who loved me for exactly who I am. Sex was great, fun, and even adventurous, but what I had been truly missing (and hadn't even realized was possible) was the experience of deep unconditional love and acceptance that I now had every day. I wholeheartedly departed from the belief that daily sex was what I wanted and embraced the more profound, more sustainable kind of love we both shared and cherished. This amazing, flowing, intimate connection is the essence of Wabi Sabi Love that just gets better with time.

My friends Arjuna and Chameli knew they wanted that kind of everlasting love, so they set out from the very beginning to celebrate their intimacy with a high level of understanding and creativity to deal with their potentially explosive emotional hot buttons.

THE BENEFITS OF JEALOUSY

When Arjuna and Chameli Ardagh first met, they agreed they would have to embark on their love relationship in a completely different manner than in the past. They had both independently realized that the habits they inherited from their parents, culture, and conditioning were predisposed toward separation, judgment, conflict, criticism, control, and disappointment.

Early on in their relationship, they went on a camping trip atop the Sierra Mountains. They lit a fire under the stars and compared notes for many hours about their previous experiences of marriage and relationship. Both had experienced a lot of negativity. They had been judged, criticized, and controlled by their partners. In turn, they had done the same. They knew that for their budding relationship to work, they would have to base their love on honesty and communication from the start. They laid it all out, much like the disclaimer clause you sign when you buy a house. They resolved that if they were to be together, they would need to find ways to transform all these habits into something that served love rather than separation.

One habit that Arjuna offered up for transformation was a subtle jealousy he had experienced his whole life. We're not talking about tantrums or throwing things; his was the insidious kind of indirect jealousy, which, he tells me, British people are prone to. In previous relationships, when his partner would answer the phone and go into another room, he'd feel something tighten in his belly.

"Who were you talking to on the phone?" he'd ask casually.

"Oh, just a friend," came the reply.

Another invisible tensing. "Oh. Great." A pregnant pause. "Anyone I know?"

"No, just a friend."

Subtle as it was, and completely unfounded, this tendency toward suspicion, jealousy, and possessiveness created a tension in the relationship that prevented a deeper flow of love.

As a result, among the many agreements and practices they cooked up that night under the stars was the idea to create a fictitious character that would represent jealousy and wrath in their relationship. They christened him Luigi. Whenever this tendency toward jealousy would arise in Arjuna, he would, for five minutes, deliberately channel Luigi. He imagined Luigi was an Italian man with slicked-back, oily hair, little ringlets on his shirt collar, and a sparkling earring. He wore shiny, pointy-toed black shoes and leopard-skin pants that accentuated his sorely lacking manhood.

"Eh!" Arjuna would call out in a thick Italian accent, grabbing Chameli playfully by the arm. "Come-ah here-ah! You-ah are-ah my-ah woman! You hear-ah me? You no look at any utter man! You understand?! You look at a nutter man, I keel you bote!"

By consciously acting this way just for five minutes whenever the need arose, Arjuna quickly transformed his jealousy from a tension that could have created separation between them into something humorous that they could laugh about together. It became the bridge to the very intimacy such feelings had hindered in past relationships. In fact, Luigi kindled an even deeper attraction that Chameli found irresistible. Through this practice, they realized that jealousy itself was not the problem; it was *resisted* jealousy that had caused tension and separation in their relationships. Embracing their feelings—whether insecurity, annoyance, or fear—helped them overcome dozens of old habits. They developed similar practices to deal with those emotions as well and discovered a completely different way of being together. Their role-playing helped them be the stars in the show of their own making. Arjuna and Chameli's healthy Wabi Sabi approach to dealing with his jealousy is fun, creative, and humorous.

WABI SABI PRINCIPLE

Playfulness and role-playing keep your relationship fresh, alive, and vibrant. The cousin of humor, playfulness is not only relaxing but also nurturing as you learn and grow together.

It's said that variety is the spice of life, and yet in the world of intimate connection, we often become repetitive in how we relate. Not only our sexual relations become mechanical (you know what I mean; hand goes here, head tosses there), but also our way of interacting too.

A few years before I met Brian, my sister, Debbie, and I attended a Tantra workshop together presented by Margot Anand. When it was time to do an interactive exercise, we were told to pick a partner, so naturally Debbie and I teamed up, not knowing that within the first thirty seconds we would be asked to do things that even sisters don't necessarily want to share with each other. We were to ask the question, "Where and how do you most like to be touched?" Now remember, this was a Tantra workshop with tantric exercises. As I began to ponder this, I quickly realized that there was no way I was about to describe my sexual preferences to my sister. So we did the only sane thing two sisters could do in a situation like the one we were in. We left the seminar and went shopping!

Later on, however, I thought more about the depth of this question. I realized it was indeed an important exercise from which any romantic partnership could benefit.

Whether you've been with your partner two months or more than twenty years, I would suggest you find twenty minutes to try this exercise and do it with a strong sense of "beginner's mind."

EXERCISE: *Getting to Know You*

To create ambiance, light a few candles, but have enough light in the room so you can easily see each other. For this exercise you will sit across from each other, holding hands and looking into each other's eyes. You will take turns whispering in your partner's ear, while you answer where and how you like to be touched in each area of your body. Think carefully before you answer.

What may have previously been true for you may no longer be true. This is an opportunity to learn something new about your partner and vice versa.

Begin each answer with: I love (or like) it when you touch my _____.

(Examples: "I like it when you lightly scratch my scalp as I am falling asleep." Or, "I love it when you hold my head in your hands as you gaze into my eyes while you are kissing me.")

Take turns answering while going through this list of body parts:

Head, Face, Lips, Ears, Neck, Shoulders, Chest, Abdomen, Upper Back, Lower Back, Buttocks, Genitals, Thighs, Knees, Calves, Feet, Upper Arm, Inside of Elbow, Lower Arm, and Hands.

Do this exercise with wonder and curiosity. It's a unique opportunity to discover new and delightful ways to pleasure your beloved. What you will take away is a more profound connection and intimacy than you've ever had before.

Now I realize it's not always easy or comfortable to ask your beloved for new, better, or different ways to play in the bedroom. And if you don't think your partner will be open to the exercise above, you can begin by asking a simple question that will quickly open the door for your partner to then ask you for your preferences; the question is: "Is there anything I can do for you now that will make you smile from ear to ear?"

Bringing a sense of fun and enthusiasm to sex helps lighten the mood when we are feeling apprehensive around getting our desires met. When Brian and I first got together, I always made sure we had lots of candles lit before we made love. Being a candle lover long before I met Brian, I would sometimes light candles to bathe by or to enjoy them while watching TV in bed. I remember early on in our relationship he walked into the bedroom late one night, after a very long drive back from Los Angeles. He spotted the tea lights and said in a tired and confused voice, "Oh, I didn't realize you were in the mood." I quickly realized that he had associated candles to canoodling and assured him I was just enjoying the vanilla scent and the soothing light and that I wasn't trying to seduce him. That night he learned that candles don't always lead to sex and that sex does not always come with candles!

EIGHT

Wabi Sabi Oneness

In love the paradox occurs that two beings become
one and yet remain two.—*Erich Fromm*

Where does our yearning to be connected to another come
from? What is the innate desire to share our lives with
someone? Is it simply a wish to overcome our feelings of
loneliness and sense of separateness? To have our lives witnessed? Or, is it in our DNA to be mated?

Many years ago I heard an intriguing story that origi-
nated at Plato's Symposium where Aristophanes, the
acclaimed comic playwright and philosopher of ancient
Athens, offered a wild tale about how our deep desire for

Oneness came about. The story is a bit graphic, but warrants retelling here.

According to the old Greek philosopher, human beings were once spherical with eight limbs. Like octopuses, they had four arms and four legs, one head with two faces and four ears, and two sets of genitals, male or female, or a combination of both, so there were three kinds of beings: male-male, male-female, and female-female.

These beings rolled through life in constant ecstasy, which managed to seriously offend the gods, especially Zeus. According to the story, Zeus feared that these happily blissful beings were not duly subservient to the all-powerful gods, so he decided to punish them. They were cut in half and their severed parts were then scattered in opposite directions.

Since that day, we mere mortals, who were once upon a time rolling balls of united joy, have been searching for our other halves.

This would certainly explain why we become deliriously happy and overjoyed with the promise of new love and delight when one half finally does meet its counterpart. It is an expression of our original state of union. We believe, at least for a while, that we are complete now that we are reunited with our other half, thus obtaining "wholeness."

The first time I heard this story, I felt tremendous resonance with it.

Yes, this is the truth, I thought. *I do yearn for my other half because he is indeed a missing piece of my soul.*

So, what does it take to create a magnificent relationship that grows in the face of adversity and nurtures and sustains two souls (and the entire family, community, and, quite possibly, the world)?

It's not magic, yet it is a magical process. While adjoining ourselves with our soulmates may be a natural experience, bringing two hearts into harmony and alignment for a lifetime of love is not something we are hardwired to know how to do.

Learning to happily coexist with your other half is a bit like the process of a pearl coming into being. For millennia many cultures such as the Persians, Chinese, and Hindus have treasured pearls for their great beauty. Pearls have been thought to represent great love, prosperity, and goodness. Natural pearls, which are very rare and occur in only one oyster or mussel out of a thousand, result from a primal irritation, often a parasite or larvae that invades the mollusk. Imagine your relationship to be like a seedling growing into a pearl . . . an irritation that over time transforms into a thing of great beauty, much prized for the light it shines into the world.

For you more practical types, think of it this way: You buy a new pair of leather shoes. They are stiff in the beginning, and they will possibly give you a blister or two, but once you break them in, they become your favorites and you want to wear them all the time!

Just as we sometimes get blisters when we wear new shoes, change can also bring unwanted, yet very helpful, pain that makes us stand up and take notice.

TRUE LOVE: A HUG AND A REALITY CHECK

Claire is a beautiful, single Australian who moved to northern California in 2002 to pursue a Ph.D. in transformative learning and, more important, to follow an inner feeling that she was meant to live in America. On top of this major move, she was recovering from a broken heart and a series of disasters. She claims she consciously brought on these situations with "a clear desire to accelerate all of my personal issues so that I could grow and expand on every level and become the teacher I was destined to be."

Within one month her dog died in her arms, her business fell apart, she lost her home, and her boyfriend dumped her. She found herself sleeping on a blow-up mattress at her mom and dad's house. Nearly suicidal, traumatized, and in the midst of her dark night of the soul, thinking positively was nearly impossible.

One Wednesday afternoon while rock climbing, hanging off the edge of a cliff, she heard a voice say, "Can you say yes to life even though you are in so much pain?"

Her simple and truthful response was that she didn't know.

During the next three months as she pondered the possibility of saying yes to life, she came to a life-altering conclusion: "I can say yes to life by choosing to be a presence of love in this world in spite of my pain."

With renewed energy for life, Claire became determined to do whatever she needed to do to become the woman she was meant to be. Her decision led her to America. During the next five years, alone but focused, she dove into her studies, made new friends and connections, and began a career as a teacher of transformation.

In spite of her spiritual growth during these years, she hadn't been willing to truly open her heart again to love. One lonely night she became overwhelmed with the sense that once again she needed a mind shift. She became acutely aware that unless she shifted on a very deep level, she was likely to spend the rest of her life without ever knowing true love.

The next morning she called her best friend, Katherine, who just so happened to be an expert in the domain of creating love relationships. Claire shared that she was finally ready and open to receive love if that was indeed her destiny.

Excellent student that she is, Claire followed Katherine's directions and quickly manifested Craig, another teacher of transformation. Within six months they were engaged, and nearly a year to the date that they met, they married in a small, intimate ceremony at the Inn of the Seventh Ray in Topanga Canyon outside Los Angeles. And this is where their story begins.

In the beginning she was amazed by the similarities between them. They shared identical values about family, money, and their careers.

"It was heaven to be with someone who completely shared my sensibilities."

And then, slowly but surely as with every couple we've met, the differences between them emerged. You could call the source of their differences a culture clash. Craig had spent many years in a community dedicated to evolution in which members constantly gave one another feedback on what was working and not, challenging one another on all issues, in order to raise the consciousness of the group. Claire was working in a community of women where the feedback was mostly sweet, unconditionally loving, compassionate, and, most of all, gentle.

"Craig was freely offering his feedback on everything from my driving to how I chopped vegetables. Imagine my surprise to be receiving coaching on when and how to change lanes even though I had been driving for fifteen accident-free years without his help, thank you very much!"

Claire recalled. "Of course he said all this in the nicest possible way, but . . ."

One year after their wedding, Claire found herself working around the clock to launch a new product. It was a very challenging time business-wise. Instead of responding with much needed support, Craig was busy pointing out to her all the choices she made that had gotten her into trouble and how she could have done a better job.

As they walked to a restaurant for a lovely, potentially relaxing dinner in San Francisco one evening, Craig continued his stream of feedback on the myriad ways Claire could have and should have avoided the situation she was currently in with her product launch.

And so she announced to Craig: "You know what? I can't be in this conversation right now. It's not helping, and it's certainly not what I need right now. I need to go for a walk by myself and take a time-out."

For the next two hours Claire walked aimlessly through the streets of San Francisco. She let herself feel the deep disappointment of not getting the support she needed from her husband, and she questioned whether or not she would ever be able to get the emotional nourishment she wanted from him. She asked herself the all-important question: "Can I really live without the kind of support I've always expected to have?"

WABI SABI PRINCIPLE

Care takes many forms. Wabi Sabi Love takes an open heart and an open mind to receive your partner's deep level of care, even if it looks different from what you would expect.

And as she walked through her feelings and questions with tremendous anxiety and great despair, she had what she now realizes was a Wabi Sabi moment: "I realized that for Craig his feedback is what 'care' looks like to him."

When Claire stopped to consider the truth of his voluminous and often unsolicited feedback, she was finally able to acknowledge that he truly was supporting her in ways that were very useful. She realized that it was because of his feedback and suggestions that she had grown more as a person than at any other time in her life. She further saw that thanks to Craig's input, her career was thriving in ways that empowered her to make her greatest contribution to the world. She found her heart opening as she realized that Craig's love for her included his huge desire and commitment to her success. He was looking out for her and loving her in a way that no one else ever had.

She had expected support to look like someone who would comfort her and assure her everything would be okay rather than someone who would continually challenge her to grow and stretch. She was finally ready to admit to herself that what Craig offered her was really what she wanted and needed.

While Claire had been walking through the city, Craig had been driving around and came to a realization of his own: he truly wanted to express to Claire the depth and breadth of his commitment to her, on all levels of their relationship. And he finally saw that he needed to provide loving and supportive encouragement in addition to the direct feedback he had been giving her.

Claire ended her walk by entering a hotel in downtown San Francisco. She went in to find a pay phone to call Craig and tell him she was ready to reconnect with him and talk heart to heart about their issues. Much to their surprise, they discovered that they were standing twenty feet apart from each other in a hotel neither of them had ever been in before. The sheer synchronicity of it had them laughing hysterically, and they quickly saw that it meant they were to be together. The magic of the night was deeply transformative and solidified their Oneness as a couple.

Mythologist Joseph Campbell said it beautifully:

Marriage is not a love affair. A love affair is a totally different thing. A marriage is a commitment to that which you are. That person is literally your other half. And you and the other are one. A love affair isn't that. That is a relationship of pleasure, and when it gets to be unpleasurable, it's off. But a marriage is a life commitment, and a life commitment means the prime concern of your life. If marriage is not the prime concern, you are not married.*

Wabi Sabi Oneness is about the "we" of the relationship serving as the success and anchor as opposed to the individual "I." It's about always playing on the same team. It's about sharing and making choices that serve the highest good of the relationship. In fact, Wabi Sabi Oneness can be solidified by difference.

In the world of astrology, the sign of Gemini is known as the twins, and it is commonly accepted that Geminis see the world from two (or more) points of view. Brian is a Gemini and is able (and often willing) to take on any and all sides of a debate when he is in a feisty mood. I am a Capricorn, a mountain goat, sure-footed and steadfast in my ideas and opinions. In the zodiac, we are polar opposites. This has its advantages (some say polar opposites are a perfect match), and it also has its challenges. It took me a few years

---

*http://thinkexist.com/quotation/marriage-is-not-a-love-affair-a-love-affair-is-a/403971.html, accessed on January 31, 2011.

to understand Brian's natural ability to see multiple points of view simultaneously, while I was busy trying to persuade him to become single-focused on *my* point of view.

One of Brian's great passions in life is assisting the disenfranchised. He spends time each day walking around the city to care for and look after the ever-increasing homeless population. Many years ago I started an organization to help homeless women with children and in three years' time raised one million dollars to donate to the cause. The difference between Brian and me is that he looks forward to hanging out on the streets with those he helps, while I prefer to figure out ways to get people to write me checks that I can then give to someone else to help those on the streets.

In our second year of marriage we were planning a long trip to India. Our usual catsitter had moved away, and we were searching for the perfect person to care for our four-legged babies. Brian came home one day and announced that one of his homeless friends, Roger, had volunteered to move in and care for the cats.

Once I remembered to keep breathing, I tried, as calmly as possible, to suggest to Brian that I wasn't sure that would be a good idea. We were going to be in India for three weeks, out of touch, completely unavailable. What if something happened? What if one of the cats got sick? Or the water heater burst? Or a tidal wave came? Could this homeless man be responsible for our cats and all our stuff?

Brian calmly suggested that I meet Roger before I decide he was incapable of looking after things.

In my mind, we were definitely on the verge of a potentially big problem. I had met some of Brian's friends who lived on the streets. Some were quite chatty and intelligent, while others were clearly not entirely in their right mind. I was imagining the worst.

The next afternoon the doorbell rang—and there was Brian's friend, Roger, a sixty-something balding jock, wearing khaki shorts, a T-shirt, and running shoes, who looked like he could be somebody's grandfather. He shook my hand and began talking nonstop about the wonderful things he had heard about me from Brian. I quickly learned that he was a retired Boeing engineer who loved to play senior softball nearly every day. He described himself as "cheap," which was why he liked living in his van rather than "wasting money" on rent. Within minutes I realized that Roger was a different kind of homeless than the picture I had constructed in my mind. For the next several years, until he retired to the Seattle area, Roger was our beloved catsitter. This experience taught me that just because someone does not have a traditional home doesn't mean I shouldn't view the person with the same respect I have for everyone else.

But the bigger lesson for me was learning to trust Brian's judgment. I quickly discovered he would never, ever put me (or the cats) in harm's way.

The Chinese parable that follows speaks to the importance of never making assumptions about outward appearances. Just as I was ready to judge Roger as irresponsible based on his living situation, I quickly learned that he had created a "home" that worked for him. We ended up with a trusted friend to stay in our home so that we could be free to travel. Sometimes imperfection is actually perfection at work in disguise.

An elderly Chinese woman had two large pots; they hung on opposite ends of a pole, which she carried across the back of her neck. One of the pots had a crack in it, while the other pot was perfect and always delivered a full portion of water. At the end of the long walk from the stream to the house, the cracked pot arrived only half full. For a full two years this went on daily, with the woman's bringing home only one and a half pots of water.

Of course, the perfect pot was proud of its accomplishments. But the poor cracked pot was ashamed of its own imperfection and miserable that it could only do half of what it had been made to do. After two years of what it perceived to be bitter failure, it spoke to the woman one day by the stream.

"I am ashamed of myself because this crack in my side causes water to leak out all the way back to your house."

The old woman smiled, "Did you notice that there are flowers on your side of the path, but not on the side of the other pot? Because I have always known about your flaw, I planted flower seeds on your side of the path, and every day while we walk back, you water them. For two years I have been able to pick these beautiful flowers to decorate the table. Without your being just the way you are, there would not be this beauty to grace the house."

Each of us has a unique flaw. But it's the particular cracks and flaws that each one of us brings that make our lives together so interesting and rewarding. Like puzzle pieces that fit just so, our edges and curves help us form a bond that would not have been possible otherwise. When you take all people for what they are, it is easier to find the good in each one's singularity.

Sometimes the perceived flaw can be the pursuit of perfection, which can turn out to be the best thing of all. Unlike many couples of their generation, Bob and Tricia were a bit "old-fashioned" and chose not to live together until they formally married seventeen years ago. Deeply in love after a two-year courtship, Bob never imagined there were things about Tricia he didn't know that would come to surprise him once they were man and wife.

WHEN NOTHING LESS THAN PERFECT WILL DO

Bob loves the creativity and the precision of his days as a filmmaker, whether it's screenwriting, producing, or directing. When he's working, he demands perfection. But when he comes home from work, he likes to leave the structure far behind and relax into a casual, free and easy lifestyle. Once they married, Bob discovered that Tricia could only relax when everything was "as it should be," whether that meant all the towels were matching and hanging *just so* on the rack or her hair was correctly in place. (From Bob's point view, Tricia had great hair every day. However, Tricia's mood was seriously affected by whether or not *she* felt she was having a good hair day.)

Most days Bob learned to go with the flow when it came to Tricia's need for perfection, even when he became the focus of it. There were some days, however, when he did wish he could change her more obsessive tendencies. He remembers one incident that occurred on a drive to San Diego to see his in-laws.

"We stopped for gas, and I was feeling hungry, so I bought a bag of sour cream potato chips. Tricia immediately said to me, 'That's not lunch, is it? Do you know how many grams of fat are in there'?"

She knew the calorie and fat content of absolutely everything. At the time Bob ripped open that bag of chips, he had no way of knowing that this particular talent of hers, while occasionally annoying, would eventually prove lifesaving.

Like many young couples, Bob and Tricia were excited to begin a family. And while it took longer than they expected, they were thrilled when she was finally pregnant with the assistance of a fertility expert. Tricia began painting, planning, and readying the nursery.

One evening Bob came home to find an ambulance in front of the house just as Tricia was being wheeled out on a stretcher. Terrified, he raced to her side. She was in horrible pain and was quickly rushed to the hospital.

As the doctor scanned her abdomen in a pitch-black room, he soon determined that she had flipped an ovary and that is what had caused the pain. The doctor continued to stare at the screen studying two very obvious dark spaces.

Bob quietly asked, "Are they twins?"

"Yes, and I'm trying to figure out if it may be triplets," said the doctor.

A few minutes later it was confirmed that they were pregnant with triplets. The fertility doctor then dropped one more bombshell on the already shocked couple. He suggested that they eliminate one of the triplets and told Tricia that she was an excellent candidate for a "reduction." As a therapist, Tricia had witnessed firsthand the pain and discord decisions like these had caused couples who were faced with potential consequences of a high-risk pregnancy. It wasn't the actual decision to reduce the pregnancy that tore them apart. It was when couples chose to have the babies, who were quite often born with genetic disorders. The financial stress and time intensity of such care was the thing that ruined many a marriage. In a separate conversation, their delivery doctor also expressed his concern about the health of their babies and what that might do to their marriage. Despite both doctors' warnings, Bob and Tricia's spiritual beliefs led them to embrace their babies' existence without hesitation and went home to prepare themselves for the unexpected added blessings.

Tricia, ever the good patient, scheduled regular appointments, and at week fifteen went in for her checkup. Surrounded by the delivery doctor they loved and the nurses they felt really comfortable with, they noticed that the look on the doctor's face indicated that something was really, really wrong. The doctor urgently explained to them that Tricia's body was going into labor and in order to save the babies, she had to go on complete bed rest.

The doctor was adamant: "You have to give me three perfect months of total bed rest so I can deliver three perfect babies. This means no walks, no movies, no nothing. You can only get out of bed to go to the bathroom and to shower once a day."

Bob began to research all the possible ways they could support Tricia and their three tiny babies. He discovered a special diet for multiple pregnancies known as Brewer Diet, which required mom-to-be Tricia, a 106-pound, life-long finicky eater to not only consume a wide variety of foods she didn't love, but to also plan on gaining sixty pounds.

"Honey, thank God you're a perfectionist. We need you to diligently track and monitor every glass of water and every mouthful of food to keep you and our babies healthy and strong," Bob explained.

Bob, with impeccable devotion, cooked her every meal, and Tricia willingly ate and drank everything he brought to her. Bob fed her all kinds of hearty foods such as feta cheese omelets, ice cream shakes, steak, and turkey burgers. She washed down every meal with buckets of water. They both clearly understood what was at stake, and they were counting on her perfectionism to save the lives of their three unborn children.

The doctor continued to make them aware of the risks and potential dangers of their situation. He carefully explained that they had to make it to twenty-four weeks, which happened to be Labor Day, or he would insist on a reduction, which was something they definitely did not want to consider.

"I am not worried about your losing your babies. I am worried about the strong possibility that one or more of them will be born with a genetic disorder and that the stress of raising them will destroy your marriage."

Bob believed in his heart that their marriage was strong enough to handle whatever the outcome. Tricia listened to hymns, and they both prayed daily. Their family and friends were also praying and supporting them.

On Labor Day, Tricia's contractions went crazy. They rushed to the doctor's office, where she was wheeled in on a stretcher. Before the doctor had a chance to examine her, Tricia told him, "I'm not giving up. We're committed to this."

The doctor was wary. He told them that any movement at all would put the babies at risk of being born prematurely. His prescription? "We need two more perfect months."

Tricia and Bob promised the doctor they could comply with two more perfect months of complete bed rest. They would do anything for the sake of their precious angels. In the end, they managed to make it to week thirty-five before the doctor performed a C-section. All three babies came out at around three pounds each. Although they were small, they were absolutely perfect.

Deliriously happy, tired, and relieved, Bob was right there to cut all the cords.

The triumph of his wife's efforts to follow the doctor's orders precisely showed Bob the positive side of Tricia's perfectionism. To this day Bob is, and will be forever, grateful that he married Tricia, for he believes in his heart that it was her perfectionism that saved all three of their beautiful babies. "Once we settled in at home and began taking care of them, I became even more appreciative that she is exactly who she is," he shared. "The task of caring for and feeding three babies demands an amazing degree of organization and precision to keep track of all the feedings, diaper changes, and the zillion other crazy details that come up raising and nurturing triplets."

Bob and Tricia's lives are full and happy, thanks in large part to developing a love of perfection—and each other. Through this experience the couple emerged as a strong team, fully immersed in love, trust, and gratitude.

For those of you who are thinking that this story, which sings the praises of perfection, sounds like a contradiction of Wabi Sabi, I ask you to consider this one word: paradox. A paradox is something that seems like a contradiction but actually expresses a nondual truth. Wabi Sabi is the art of finding beauty and perfection in imperfection. In the story of Bob and Tricia, the Wabi Sabiness comes from the fact that her perfectionism, which was once a major problem and stumbling block for Bob, is now honored as the very thing that brought forth the lives of their triplet sons. Maybe a better way to say it is this: that which once made you crazy now makes you grateful.

Gratitude is closely related to abundant thinking. If we are steeped in a *lack* mentality, we concentrate more on what is missing than on what we actually have. The way we view money reveals a lot about how abundant our thinking is.

Differing beliefs around the handling of money can undermine a couple's connection and even threaten their marriage. Jeffrey Dew, an assistant professor of family studies at Utah State University, found that conflict around money is a top predictor of divorce. In his research at the University of Virginia's National Marriage Project, he discovered that couples who reported having financial disagreements once a week had a 30 percent higher likelihood of divorce than couples who only disagreed about finances a couple of times a month. The money conversation is often riddled with our fears of being left destitute, alone, or uncared for. If one partner is thrifty while the other is a big spender, it can lead to disaster.

Having grown up in a family that for generations had been steeped in poverty consciousness, I was always acutely aware of what we didn't have. As a child, I remember hearing stories from both sets of grandparents about the poverty they endured during the Great Depression when both my mother and father were babies. That, coupled with my parents' endless fighting over the lack of money in our home, programmed me to both fear and desire money. As a young woman, my biggest fear was that I would end up as a bag lady. To counteract this, I became rather careful with my money. I paid my bills on time and never carried any credit-card debt. I only bought clothes and house furnishings that were on sale. If there was something special that I wanted to do or have (say, a vacation or a new car), I saved up for it. I became inordinately proud of my stellar credit rating and developed a sense of financial security.

When Brian and I got married, I was fascinated (and sometimes a little scared) by his ease with money. Even though he grew up in a home where there was always more than enough and he achieved financial success early in his career, Brian would often tell me that he would be just as comfortable living under a bridge somewhere. Yikes! Having worked with the homeless for so many years, Brian has spent a handful of nights where he chose to sleep on the streets in order to gain a deeper understanding of the lives of the disenfranchised. Gregarious, confident, and very generous, Brian takes great pleasure in taking friends out to dinner and picking up the tab for everyone. When his money and my money became "our" money, I often found myself silently judging his largess. In my world, the proper thing to do would have been to equally split the check, unless it was a birthday or some other special event and it was clear that someone was the guest of honor. (Who makes these rules, by the way?)

One day I just outright asked him why he was always Quick Draw McGraw whenever the dinner check arrived. The question seemed to puzzle him for a moment, and then he simply said, "It makes my heart sing, and, more important, I believe that money is energy and that the generosity of spirit comes back to us in many different ways."

I then asked myself, *If we had split the check on those occasions, would that have made my heart sing?* The answer? Of course not! In that Wabi Sabi instant I decided to let my judgments and apprehension about the check thing return to the nothingness from whence it came. Whenever my poverty consciousness rears its cheap and insecure head from time to time, I stop for a moment, acknowledge my fear and then choose to go back to having an abundant mind-set.

Over the years we've become a loving and trusting team. Brian listens to my point of view, I listen to his, and then we make choices based on our number one priority, which is doing what is best for the relationship and ultimately serves the highest good.

Shortly after Peggy and Denis fell in love, they discovered that they each had radically divergent views about money. To their credit, they took this Wabi Sabi opportunity to blend each of their unique financial strengths into a unified approach that gives them both peace of mind.

LOVE, MONEY, AND SAFETY NETS

When they first started living together, Denis asked Peggy some very direct questions about money and her business. Anyone will tell you that there's a definite difference between being asked a few casual questions and undergoing a full-blown interrogation. The tone of Denis's voice made Peggy feel like she was sitting in an airless basement room under a lone lightbulb, if you know what I mean. As a result, she had a sinking suspicion that her new husband must not trust her decisions with money.

At the time, she owned the house in which they lived. A born entrepreneur, Peggy owned and operated a flourishing consulting business. Although business was very good, Denis would pose questions such as: "What happens when the business isn't doing very well?" "What will you do if you are not making any income?" and "What is your backup plan?"

Having met Denis in her forties, Peggy was accustomed to taking care of her financial responsibilities on her own. She had a successful business that earned her a very healthy income. Sure, being an entrepreneur involves financial risk, but her belief system was based on trust and an appropriate commitment to fulfilling her financial obligations with ease and harmony. In short, she had an attitude of financial abundance, not one of fear or lack.

A cautious person by nature, Denis had been trained as a military pilot who never stepped aboard a plane without a backup plan. What he perceived as smart thinking landed on Peggy's ears as negativity. She emphasized possibility; he emphasized caution.

Peggy's interpretation of his probing questions was that he didn't trust or believe in her. On some level, she felt attacked and surprised by his relentlessness about financial matters.

Over dinner one evening, she decided to get to the bottom of it all.

Gently broaching the subject, Peggy asked Denis why he was so concerned about money since they were both doing well financially. Denis revealed that in his previous marriage his wife had been very irresponsible with money. He described how she once spent twice her salary in a year, heaping a substantial financial burden on their already wavering relationship. Her reckless spending habits created severe tension in their marriage, something he never wanted to repeat. Since Denis was trained to have a backup plan, he needed some reassurance that everything would be fine in the event that, due to an accident or illness, Peggy couldn't earn an income. His biggest apprehension was that he would have to carry the entire financial burden if she wasn't able to contribute. His concern didn't stem from distrust or a lack of belief in Peggy's business decisions; he simply needed assurances that things were in place to give him peace of mind.

As she mulled over their conversation, Peggy had a tremendous realization a few nights later. Snuggling on the couch while watching a televised hockey game and enjoying their favorite deli pizza, Peggy suddenly realized that their combined points of views on handling money offered them something of incredible value: long-term security and peace of mind. She saw that her positive attitude toward always having an abundance of money meshed beautifully with Denis's caution. He not only had a plan A; he also had a plan B. He was trained and prepared in the event of unexpected challenges.

Two great things came from the couple's money dialogue: respect and a long-term vision. When Peggy realized the origin of Denis's cautiousness about money, she purchased three types of insurance and made some investments to provide a greater safety net. She also learned to respect Denis's own beliefs about money without trying to convert him to her way of thinking. Peggy and Denis's story shows how even the morass of the money relationship can offer an opportunity to strengthen the marital one.

Brian and I have always shared a dream that one day we would become philanthropists. We both enjoy supporting good causes, and I like to think of us as "major philanthropists in training."

One of the ways we plan to fund this dream is by winning the lottery. You may remember from the introduction that my grandma Ada won part of the Irish sweepstakes, and I am holding out hope that her good luck runs in the family. As a result, we often buy lottery tickets. I like to purchase the Quick Pick while Brian prefers to buy our lucky numbers. When we first began doing this, I had a sleepless night when I started thinking about all the things that could go wrong if we really won (It's true . . . even after years of therapy, workshops, and self-help books, I still have my neurotic moments).

What if we fought about how to spend the money? What if strangers started showing up at the front door with their hands out?

I had read all the stories about the ruin and demise of lottery winners, and I wanted to make sure that it didn't happen to us. We've had many lively conversations on this subject, because we are highly aware of the impact money can have on a marriage. Luckily, we made an agreement in advance about how we plan to distribute the winnings.

Just for fun, try this with your partner and see what happens:

Get a dollar bill. Take turns asking each other to write down what you would do with it. Now increase the amount by ten. Repeat the exercise until you get to one million dollars. Discuss the results. Practice listening without filtering your partner's response with your own belief system about money. If objections come up in your mind, notice them, then let them go. Use this as an exercise to start to learn more about where your partner's attitudes about money came from. Simply understanding the origins of his or her money beliefs can decrease pressure without necessarily warranting any changes in how you handle money together.

EXERCISE: *Reconnecting with Your Love and Clearing Disagreements*

Buy a small journal and begin an "acknowledgment diary." Every time your mate does or says something that you love, appreciate, or feel inspired by, write it in the journal so you don't forget it. Then, on a regular basis, share these acknowledgments with your partner by reading the journal out loud to him or whispering it in his ear. Before you feel you have to sit down with your partner for a big discussion about money, the kids, or whatever else, read the journal to refresh your memory about all the reasons why you love your partner.

Noted marriage researcher Dr. John Gottman has found that happily married couples disagree just as much as couples who divorce. The difference is in how the disagreements are handled. According to Gottman, it's imperative to avoid the following four major patterns when discussing differences:

Criticism (attacking the other's character)

Contempt (conveying disgust)

Defensiveness (blaming or counterattacking your partner's character)

Stonewalling (disengaging, withdrawing)

In addition, it's important to choose the right time for a discussion. Being tired, hungry, or on a work deadline, or if the kids are around are indicators that it is not a good time. Begin with mutual respect and affection, and plan to speak and listen from the heart. Bring up whatever issues you're experiencing, gently, softly, and calmly, beginning with "I felt ___" rather than the accusatory "You did ____." Agree to explore rather than solve. Research has shown that 70 percent of issues don't need to be resolved; they just need to be well discussed. The first three minutes are critical. More than 95 percent of the time, the way the discussion starts determines how it will go for the remainder of the conversation.

Wabi Sabi Love is about responsibility, trust, and oneness. It calls upon us to be responsible for the care and nurturing of each other, on all levels—body, mind, and spirit—and to honor the marriage vows of "in sickness and in health." Wabi Sabi Oneness means being on the same team, standing behind each other's successes, and trusting who you are in the world as a couple. Being responsible for the financial health of the family and for the everyday details of living together falls under this category. Other examples include parenting, taking care of aging parents, being a member of the community, and, ultimately, your place in the world at large.

EXERCISE: *Experiencing Oneness*

Two of my favorite relationship experts, Gay and Kathlyn Hendricks, have revealed research that proves that a twenty-second hug is the fastest way to deeply connect with your partner. A twenty-second hug releases the bonding hormone and neurotransmitter oxytocin. Known as the hormone of love and cuddling, oxytocin is nature's antidepressant and antianxiety hormone. It creates feelings of calm and a sense of connection, so it actually shapes how you view the world. The whole universe looks like a better place when you are feeling tranquil and loving. Who wouldn't want more of that?

The purpose of this exercise is to connect deeply on a heart level with your partner and experience your Oneness. To begin, join your partner in a twenty-second (or longer) deep, melting hug by standing heart-to-heart, with your arms around each other and your hands placed on each other's backs in the area near the heart. The idea is to get as close as possible while still being comfortable. Breathe gently yet deeply, and if it feels right, add some sound effects . . . a few hmms, yums, or sighs will enhance the experience.

Then, when you are finishing hugging, sit across from each other, either in two chairs, knee to knee or cross-legged on the floor.

Hold hands and begin by gently placing your attention on yourself.

Observe how your body is feeling.

Notice your breathing . . . are you breathing quickly, slowly, from your mouth or nose? Feel the temperature of the room around you.

Next, let your awareness flow from yourself to your partner and notice something about her body. Notice the rise and fall of her chest as she breathes. See if you can sense where in her body she is holding tension. Feel the warmth of his hands. Begin to gaze into his eyes . . . not like a staring contest but gaze with the eyes of love allowing yourself to blink or look away as needed. Allow yourself to see him anew as he is seeing you in a new and unique way.

Next, begin to synchronize your breathing with her breathing as best you can. This will bring the two of you into coherence and Oneness.

Imagine your heart opening and sending her silent messages of love, appreciation, and gratitude. Then bring your attention back to yourself and see if you can receive the silent messages of love, appreciation, and gratitude that she is sending back to you.

For many of us it is easier to give than to receive, so allow oneself to open, soften, and welcome in these precious gifts that our partners are giving us. Spend five minutes (or more) together, sending and receiving love, in silence, with the intention of experiencing the pure joy of remembering your Oneness.

Like many couples that have been together for a long time, Brian and I often finish each other's sentences. But we sometimes find ourselves in a state of awe with our ability to communicate telepathically. Even though Brian refuses to own a cell phone, we are never really out of touch. If I need to talk to him, I just close my eyes and send him the thought to call or e-mail me, and generally within minutes I hear from him. Our unspoken communication shows up in other ways as well. We live in a very old house with small rooms. My closet is in the master bedroom, and Brian's is in the guest room. When we are in our respective dressing rooms, we randomly select our clothes for the day without any prior conversation. Nine days out of ten, when we see each other, we are wearing the same color and it appears that we have coordinated our outfits! It's another way we seem to mystically stay in sync!

Even as we intersect with each other on many levels, we remain individuals with our unique views of the world. Wabi Sabi Oneness is not codependence, but the expression of two strong individuals blending each other's lives into one loving cocreation.

NINE

The Personal Art of Happiness

Love does not dominate; it cultivates.
—*Johann Wolfgang von Goethe*

I was about to nod off on the stuffy, crowded airplane as the flight attendant began her safety demonstration. Snapping the seat-belt buckle tightly, then releasing the latch with practiced deftness, she smiled down the aisle of the airless cabin and against the wall of inattention most frequent fly-ers typically exude. The bright yellow vest around her slender frame blurred my vision, so I shut my eyes in hopes that sleep would come. Her southern drawl, coupled with the vibration of the idling plane, lulled me into a mild coma when something she said actually caught my attention:

"In the event of a sudden loss of cabin pressure, oxygen masks will descend from the ceiling. Put your own mask on first before attempting to help anyone else."

Having logged hundreds of thousands of air miles in my lifetime, I have heard that line more times than I can count and on every commercial flight I have ever been on. But that day, crammed into a window seat overlooking the rolling tarmac, I really heard it.

In order to help someone else, I first had to take care of myself. I first needed to have enough oxygen in my own mind and body before I could even think about giving anyone assistance, help, or care. As I pondered this seemingly new information, I realized that when I chose to skip my workout to meet a work deadline, or rushed through a less-than-ideal meal to save time for something I deemed more important that my own nutrition, or stayed up late writing a proposal for a potential new client, I was not contributing to that which was my highest good. What I had were seemingly good excuses for not taking the time and energy to nurture and care for myself. In my naïveté I believed that putting myself first meant that I was selfish, self-centered, or, dare I say it, egotistical.

When Brian and I first began living together, I began to notice his patterns. Every morning he would wake up happy somewhere between 4:30 and 6:00 A.M. He would make his coffee, eat a small breakfast, read the paper, and then go for a run and workout for around two hours. At least six days a week. And most days he would do a shorter workout in the afternoon as well. He also found time to meditate and do volunteer work, and he never missed a meal. Brian was and is one of the most consistent people I have ever met. I soon discovered that Brian already knew that by focusing on taking care of himself—body, mind, and spirit—he fills himself up and has more to give me and everyone around him. This is a man who smiles in his sleep. Really!

Through observation and osmosis, I began to adopt some of Brian's consistency. No, I will never work out two hours a day, but I do finally exercise nearly every day, and I have learned that peace of mind, good health, and overall happiness are the result of putting myself first.

All too often we look to the other person in our relationships to provide everything we need or our keys to happiness. But by looking within and realizing the power we have over our own circumstances, we pave the way for a happier and healthier relationship.

RULE 1: MAKE YOURSELF HAPPY

Michelle's family often worried over her chances of ever finding the right guy to marry. Beautiful, tall, athletic, smart, funny, with an Ivy League education to boot, she was superpicky when it came to the men she dated. Her brother warned her that she never gave anyone a chance.*

"You chew them up and spit them out because they never measure up to Dad."

Always willing to defend herself, Michelle told him more than once: "It's my life. You have got to stop worrying about me. I'm not looking for Dad, and I'm not about to settle either. The right guy is out there. I'll know him when I see him."

Michelle was one of a handful of African-American attorneys at the prestigious Chicago firm of Sidley & Austin when she was assigned to oversee a Harvard first-year law student who was soon arriving to become a summer associate. She had heard via the water cooler that he was good-looking with a towering intellect, but she had already decided that she was giving up dating to focus on her career.

Before the arrival of her new responsibility, she read his impressive bio and came to the conclusion that she would be spending the summer babysitting an intellectual nerd. And the nerd had a very strange name: Barack Obama.

Over lunch that first day, Michelle quickly discovered that Barack was funny, self-deprecating, and down-to-earth

---

*Many thanks to Christopher Andersen, author of *Barack and Michelle: Portrait of an American Marriage*, for his permission to use his work as the basis of this story.

despite his exotic background of being biracial and having been raised in Hawaii and Indonesia.

Barack recalls that he was instantly attracted to Michelle—her laugh, her height, and her beauty. Quite simply, they clicked. Even so, Michelle made it very clear that she had big plans, was on the fast track, and had no time for distractions, especially men.

For the next month Barack relentlessly pursued her, asking her out on a daily basis, sending her notes and flowers, and flirting with her at every opportunity. And still she resisted him.

Everything changed one Sunday morning when she accompanied him to a community meeting in a church basement and sat spellbound as he delivered an impassioned speech about "the world as it is and the world as it should be."

By now she had spent enough time with him to know that he was an exceptional human being, but to witness and experience the care and compassion he had for the world deeply touched her. She even thought, *I'd like to be married to somebody who felt that deeply about things.*

They shared a vision of wanting to improve the lives of their fellow African-Americans by getting them better health care, housing, and education. Barack confided in Michelle his belief that he could be a catalyst for change via politics.

They finally began dating, and by the end of the summer, when Barack returned to Harvard Law School, they were a fully committed couple.

They married in 1992 and began building a life together in Chicago. Michelle was the major breadwinner, while Barack began his political career. Several of their biggest issues surfaced early: They both had major debt in the form of student loans. While she handled the family finances, he was downright cavalier with money. He was also a chain-smoker and a slob. He thought nothing of leaving his clothes strewn about and wet towels on the floor.

Several years later, after Barack had been elected as an Illinois state senator, their marriage was at a breaking point.

While he was heavily engaged in his political career in Springfield, Michelle was in Chicago, working full-time, raising two young girls, and home alone each night, feeling tired, angry, abandoned, overworked, and out of shape. She was also very concerned that they would have to someday file for bankruptcy.

"He seems to think he can just go out there and pursue his dream and leave all the heavy lifting to me," she complained to her mother.

From Barack's point of view, he was focused on the big picture and felt that many of her complaints were petty.

"I love Michelle," he shared with his grandmother "Toot," "but she's killing me with this constant criticism."

They were at a crisis point.

Early one morning around 4:30, as Barack lay next to her soundly asleep, Michelle suddenly realized that if she simply got up and went to the gym to reclaim her workouts, he would be forced to take care of the kids when they got up. She tiptoed out and headed for the gym. Sure enough when she returned, the girls were fed and all was well.

From that day on, whenever Barack was home, this became her new routine.

Michelle began to take a new approach to the problems in her marriage. She had been waiting for Barack to make her happy. But as the saying attributed to Sister Mary Tricky goes, "If you really want to be happy, no one can stop you." Michelle had been waiting for Barack to be the one to change, but she now saw that she had to stop being mad at him and start problem solving. Slowly but surely, she began to cobble together the resources she needed to make herself happy. That meant finding ways to create more time and space for herself.

Michelle finally took her mother up on her long-standing offer to help her take care of the kids. She also found a new job with higher pay and less stress. Being married to a politician certainly required some sacrifice, but just as often she told her husband, "I'm not doing this by myself."

She insisted that Sundays be reserved as family day and that Barack make the time to be actively involved in the girls' lives, attending parent-teacher conferences and recitals. She brought structure where chaos once reigned.

In the midst of these changes Michelle had an epiphany: she remembered the guy she fell in love with and re-embraced their shared dreams of positively influencing the lives of millions.

With the same determination she had brought to everything in life, she found a way to live this dream while keeping herself, her marriage, and her family happy and fulfilled.

WABI SABI PRINCIPLE

Wabi Sabi Love calls for personal responsibility in which we nurture and care for ourselves as well as our partners, in mind, body, and spirit.

In her widely acclaimed, bestselling book *Spiritual Divorce*, my sister, Debbie, explains it this way: "Most of us are looking to have our emotional, physical, financial and spiritual needs met by this one person whom we have deemed special. It's often an impossible task for those given the giant responsibility of making us happy."

As Michelle Obama discovered, it's about knowing that our happiness is up to us. Our happiness resides within us, and the choices we make, like the one to put our own oxygen mask on first, lie within our realm of responsibility. It is a noble quest to become the source of our own happiness, and it requires deep listening to the requests whispered by our souls.

Sometimes the journey to our own happiness takes us through valleys and dark passages. Laura found her way back to joy in the most unexpected manner.

WRAPPED IN THE ARMS OF SURRENDER

"I don't love you anymore. I am not sure I ever did."

Moments before he left to take the family trash to the dump one life-changing evening at the start of summer, Laura's husband of fifteen years quietly relayed his message to her as he clutched the last of the garbage bags. As she peered out into the achingly beautiful vistas of Big Sky country in Montana, she reacted unlike any ordinary all-American gal. Her response could have ranged from heart-stopping tears to roof-raising rage. Instead, she steadied herself, held up a stop sign to the fearful thoughts attempting to creep in, and surprised him with the honest truth: "I don't buy it. I think this is about your own suffering."

For more than a year, Laura had watched her husband's slow and steady decline. His business was on life support, and his once toned physique was looking as depressed as she knew he was.

Laura had known this man more than half her life. She knew him to be a great guy, an attentive father who had always been loyal, loving, and supportive despite his recent atypical behavior of staying out till all hours of the night. She considered the possibility that he was having an affair, a thought that had screamed in her ear more than once. Despite her suspicions, she deliberately chose to believe him when he said he was not.

In her mind they were a happily married couple most of the time. They shared and supported each other's dreams, living an idyllic life in Montana on twenty acres while consciously raising their two kids amid a life full of dogs, horses, gardening, and adventure travel.

But now her husband was turning the family upside down.

"I just don't know if I have anything left for you," he told her when they sat down to discuss the future.

He told her he felt stuck. Desperate. Like he literally couldn't breathe. Wrestling with his misery, all he wanted was to be alone in an apartment away from his family. At that moment, he was convinced that his children would understand. After all, they wanted to see him happy, right?

Laura sucked in the cool mountain air as she considered what he said. As difficult as it was to hear, she knew on the deepest level that her husband's pain, despair, and problems were not hers to solve. Remaining calm, inside and out, she replied, "What can we do to give you the distance you need, without hurting the family?"

Blind with despair, he didn't understand her question at all. All he knew was he had to move out.

"You need an adventure," she offered, presenting him with a gold medal list of options: Take a walkabout like the aborigines; go trekking in Nepal; buy a drum set; organize a fishing trip to Alaska; camp on the beach in Baja; turn the garage into a man cave.

Although he was able to consider removing himself from his family, he voiced his concern about abandoning his business partner. His protests, along with other excuses, shut down all further talk about any type of adventure therapy.

Determined to remain as centered as possible, Laura Googled "responsible separation" and showed him what it would take to set up a responsible separation if he really wanted to move out. It involved everything from who would get to use which credit cards to how to best deal with communications. The reality of what it would take to move out sunk in. For a time, her husband no longer spoke of it.

And thus began the new normal for their family. Laura explained to her children that "Daddy's having a hard time." She continued to make the usual plans for barbecues, the Fourth of July, and hiking and boating with friends. Her husband, now officially Mr. Unreliable, continued to stay out late, miss family outings, sleep on the porch till nearly noon, and disappear suddenly without calling. Laura had her standards. She wasn't going to put up with abuse or go into denial, and she wasn't going to live like this forever. But she felt that if she gave him some room, he would be more likely to work through what she instinctively felt was a crisis of his own soul. Still, it wasn't easy. "His not calling was the hardest behavior of all to handle," Laura said. "That overt lack of respect was something completely new to me. But I knew that I didn't have to take it personally. What I knew was this was about him."

She confided in her closest friends, some of whom encouraged her to "throw the bum out and get a lawyer." And yet, Laura knew this was not personal. This was not about her. The love of her life was in meltdown, and it was now her job to hold the highest vision of their relationship even during this tumultuous period in their lives.

WABI SABI PRINCIPLE

To abbreviate suffering, practice empathy, compassion, and surrender for both yourself and your partner.

You see, Laura had recently committed to a nonnegotiable contract within herself to "the end of suffering." With the guidance of a wise and caring therapist and a stack of inspirational books by her bedside, she had arrived at a new realization: personal happiness is not based on things outside our control. By taking full responsibility for her own happiness, she now knew she could choose happiness even when, and especially if, her husband had dropped the bomb claiming he no longer loved her. Even if he didn't choose to be in their relationship in the end, this was a time to practice extreme self-care. In order to do that, she had to let go of the outcome. "There's nothing like a crisis to inspire us to practice whatever it is we practice in the way of well-being."

The question begs asking: how on earth does one reach this state of semi-enlightenment that prevents such potentially devastating news from taking a person down?

Laura summarized her approach using three concepts: You need empathy, compassion, and surrender. Through it all, you take it one breath at a time.

Laura could not only feel her husband's pain, but she also had her own deep and intimate relationship with suffering. In 2004, she survived a triple-whammy knockdown punch. As the author of fourteen unpublished novels, she finally had a publisher dangle a promising contract in front of her only to have it disappear at the last minute. It was easily the biggest rejection of her career. Shortly thereafter, her dog died, which was followed by the most devastating loss of her life: the death of her beloved father, who had been her strongest advocate.

A natural-born survivor and lifelong seeker, Laura started asking herself some of life's most important questions: *Who am I? What is my purpose?*

"This is why I became a writer," she admitted. "I want to climb into other people's shoes to discover who they are, which leads me to find out more about me. My author's statement is that I write to provide relief for myself and others. Not having that trajectory met for so many years was very painful. But I finally realized I needed to change my relationship with pain."

By 2008 when her husband's issues surfaced, Laura was well poised to "not suffer." She had come to a deep understanding of her own anguish and the destructive nature of victim thoughts. She made a conscious choice to not do this to herself or to her children.

"It's about the power of creating your present moment. I now know that you can create misery or joy. You can open the window and breathe in fresh air, or you can indulge your darkest thoughts and let circumstances inform your mood."

Determined to keep family life as happy and normal as possible, Laura created a season of summer fun for the kids and kept her sanity by writing down the thoughts and emotions of the often moment-to-moment uncertainty of her marriage. While she couldn't forecast the outcome of her husband's unpredictable state of mind, she put into practice her newly discovered life philosophy of total responsibility for her own happiness.

His erratic behavior of staying out late, going on days-long fishing trips with the guys, and leaving whenever he felt like it were nothing compared to his inability to look her in the eyes. "It was so painful to observe his downward spiral. But I knew from experience that pain can sometimes be our best guide."

In her mind, she determined she would be willing to live with uncertainty for six months.

Along the way, moments of possibility would shine through. He would water the lawn, upgrade the satellite, or join the family for dinner. Small but encouraging signs indicated to her that he might not be leaving after all and that her instincts were right. She knew he really did still love her. It was just that he didn't love himself.

In spite of these somewhat encouraging signals, she still faced challenges. One of her biggest trials revolved around *wanting* and the *attachment to outcome*:

She wanted to grow old with him.

She wanted to travel the world with him.

She wanted to see them both find success in their careers.

But it was in the wanting that her suffering lay. Laura says, "The key to climbing out of that suffering had to do with committing to the present moment and seeing that there is tremendous freedom in it. That happiness really is a choice. And it all begins with surrender."

August arrived bearing new blows. Her husband's older sister, mother of five, whose own husband of thirty years had left her for a twenty-something, was dying after a nine-year battle with cancer and needed family support. As if shaken awake by the preciousness of life, Laura's husband responded as the responsible, kind, loving person he once was by tending to his sister in her last days. From the ashes of great loss he reclaimed pieces of himself and a new appreciation for his own life. He began to see that what really matters isn't career success; what matters are relationships, especially the one with yourself. And he began to see Laura as the tremendous wife and friend she had always been.

By autumn the worst was over. He started coming home for dinner, sleeping in their bed, and making plans for the future. Four and a half months of "not buying it"—by giving him the distance he needed, not engaging in fear or drama or playing victim, but rather committing to nonsuffering with surrender—found Laura as free as she'd ever felt before.

Laura remembers their fifteenth wedding anniversary, September 25, 2008, for more than its historical significance. Laura got in the car to go pick up the kids. As she backed the vehicle away from the house, she caught a glance of her husband on the lawn mower. She recognized the very man she had married a decade and a half before as he affectionately gazed at her with a smile on his face. He tilted his head just so, mouthing the words that had been missing all summer: "I love you!"

He was back. More important, *they* were back. Love had again taken the front seat in both of their hearts for good. And she had surrender to thank for it.

Laura's story beautifully illustrates the possibility that opens up when we take personal responsibility for our hearts and our heads. By refusing to suffer, she created a space that allowed her to find beauty and perfection in the midst of what others would have surely seen as a nightmare. As Dr. Jeremy Geffen, a board-certified oncologist and pioneer in integrative medicine, elegantly explains, "The heart of healing is found in focused action and intention wrapped in the arms of surrender."

We were all raised with many misbegotten myths about "happily ever after" only to discover that our princess or knight in shining armor arrived with some serious baggage and dents. Shedding the fantasies of what we hoped our mates would be while shining a loving and bright light on the beauty of who they *really* are is the true path to happiness and contentment.

Barack and Michelle's story showed the importance of self-care and taking personal responsibility for our own happiness. Michelle taught us that we are the creators of our own joy that we can then share with our partners to multiply our sense of fulfillment. Laura's story demonstrated the healing powers of surrender and being gentle with ourselves in the darkest of moments. She assumed complete responsibility for her emotions and took the necessary steps to ensure she and her children were protected. Both stories illustrate how happiness is first found within. We must release expectations, surrender our fears, and learn that only by letting go can we let the light in.

The important question to ask yourself is not *How can I get my partner to change* but rather *Who am I being in the relationship?* Am I willing to take my attention off what's wrong with him and turn my focus on the myriad ways I can show up for him?

One way to begin this process is to actively support your partner's dreams and yearnings by practicing what Dutch researcher Caryl Rusbult at Vrije University in Amsterdam coined as the "Michelangelo effect." Like the artist Michelangelo, partners in a Wabi Sabi relationship shape each other through their interactions, eventually uncovering their ideal selves. They support those traits that promote an even more beneficial expression of who they are naturally. Just as Michelangelo believed his work as a sculptor was to reveal the figure that already existed within the stone, it is your job, as a supportive partner, to help bring out the best in your beloved. As their teammate in life, become their number one fan to encourage and nurture their every dream. To me this is an expression of unconditional love and true devotion.

One of the great things that came out of my father's obsession with football is a slightly strange family tradition that Brian and I and the rest of the family carry on to this day. Whenever one of us has a particularly big "win" in life, we sing what is now known as the Ford Family Fight Song.

It goes like this:

Hooray for Brian, Hooray for Brian
Someone's in the stands singing Hooray for Brian.
One, Two, Three, Four
Someone's gone and made a score
It's Brian, our guy!

This may sound corny, but trust me, it's fun, it feels great (whether you're the singer or the one sung to), and you can't help but feel deeply loved when someone's cheering you on.

In a relationship we all want someone with whom we can completely be ourselves. We yearn for someone who promises to love us on the good days and, more important, on the bad days too. We want someone who will be our soft place to land, who will love us for our brilliance and our neuroses, our good traits as well as the not-so-good ones. And we also want to *be* that loving, generous-hearted person to our mate.

When you find yourself noticing (or obsessing about) the cracks in your partner, close your eyes and imagine you are filling in the cracks with 24k gold. And if that doesn't work, ponder my favorite line from *A Course in Miracles*:

"The only thing that can be lacking in any situation is that which I am not giving."

Ask yourself if maybe, just maybe, the Wabi Sabi thing to do in this moment of judgment or discord is to give more acceptance, more compassion, more appreciation, more attention, more time, or more love.

The stories told throughout this book illuminate the essential truths about what happy couples do to keep the fires of love burning strong. The lessons are simple, and yet the results can be life changing.

Tell them you love and appreciate them.

Show them you care. It's the little gestures that mean everything.

Learn to love what they love: find a way to share their passion for their favorite persons, hobbies, sports, or pastimes.

Practice empathy often, and take time to feel into their feelings.

Be willing to go from annoyed to enjoyed.

Appreciate the paradoxes in yourself, your partner, and in life.

Remember to find the beauty and perfection in the imperfection. It is there, if you are willing to peer through the cracks we all possess.

The choice is ours. That is a mantra by which Brian and I now live. We can choose happiness, we can choose our attitudes about any given thing, and we can choose to leave a legacy of love, understanding, and compassion in order to impact each other and the planet in a positive, sustainable manner.

I'm glad I chose to ride off into that sunset, sometimes without the reins firmly in hand, but with an ever-loving, ever-expanding heart and a commitment to solve the mystery of happily ever after. Maybe this book will be that very manual I was missing when I first embarked on the marital adventure. It is my deepest hope that you have found inspiration and a renewed understanding of your love within its pages.

Behind the Scenes with Brian Hilliard and Arielle Ford

What manifests as an enduring, life-giving partnership is the sharing of a common life intention.
This means sharing a profound purpose in being
together. —Amara Charles

———————————————

If you spend even five minutes with Brian and Arielle, you will know they share a special bond that is sealed with laughter, mutual respect, and a deep knowing that their joined paths head off together into the sunset. Their level of honesty is both refreshing and so simple. They are the consummate Wabi Sabi couple who generously share their wisdom wherever they go.

We sat down for a brief chat to illuminate the truth behind the words in this book. Do they really walk the Wabi Sabi talk? Do they really apply these principles, make their relationship their first priority, and live in full acceptance of each other's quirks? In a word, yes! —Christine Louise Hohlbaum, author of *The Power of Slow: 101 Ways to Save Time in Our 24/7 World* and blogger for *Psychology Today*.

What is it about Arielle that makes her the One for you?

BRIAN: I started dreaming about Arielle before I met her. I was clear that there was a beautiful, powerful, wonderful women coming into my life. When we met, the two of us were incredibly aligned. I believe it was also because I was aligned with my deeper, intuitive self. Everything about our interaction told me that she was the One. I felt it so deeply. As our relationship unfolded, it was confirmed on a daily basis. The feeling was so much stronger than in any other relationship I'd had before. It blew open my heart.

What is it about Brian that makes him the One for you?

ARIELLE: I literally heard voices in my head. A voice whispered in my right ear: *This is the One. This is how this happens. This is who you will spend the rest of your life with.* I thought I was going crazy, but it was so clear. Along with it came this delicious feeling throughout my body. I was vibrating at the speed of love! Physically, I thought he was not my type because he had this perfect George Clooney haircut and preppy clothes. My body heat was reacting to him and hearing that voice clearly say he is the One really confirmed it. Once I got to know him, I learned he is the farthest thing from preppy! Thank goodness for inner voices!

Have your Wayne and Sheila moments decreased over the fourteen years you've been married or do those flare-ups still occur regularly?

BRIAN: I think they've diminished. We pay attention to those moments and have really asked ourselves, "What are the triggers and things that cause those moments?" They are more light-hearted moments than in the early part of the relationship. As a result, we've experienced an emotional, physical, and spiritual healing that helps us move out of that state much more quickly.

ARIELLE: The other thing is that we know each other so well. If I am in Sheila mode, I actually catch myself and apologize more quickly than he can even respond. He is the same way. We catch ourselves in the act! If we get sticky, it doesn't stay sticky for long, because we are willing to own our stuff.

BRIAN: Arielle makes a good point. We resolve it immediately. Arielle is like a laser. I respect that quality so much in her! In relationships in general, we all tend to sulk about things and don't communicate what we're feeling. We wander around the house, allowing our hurt feelings to fester and grow, and we end up making a mountain out of a molehill. Our magic together is the willingness to address it and to take care of it right away.

How often do you practice the twenty-second Hendricks hug?

ARIELLE: A couple of times a week, only because we are pretty affectionate all the time. But sometimes I ask for a longer hug.

BRIAN: We like to hug it out first thing in the morning, during the day, and at night. We are around each other so much that we hug each other constantly. Arielle is very good at asking for what she needs.

ARIELLE: I burrow in!

BRIAN: She asks very lovingly. I am a huge fan of hugging it out!

How have the principles of Wabi Sabi helped you in your everyday lives?

ARIELLE: For me, I don't put a lot of pressure on myself. When I mess up or forget something, rather than beat myself up, I am kinder and gentler. I let things go and beg forgiveness from people. I have less stress in my life because of Wabi Sabi. I am not a perfectionist. I am an

80–20 person. I work toward 80 percent good enough versus suffering toward perfection. It makes me more tolerant toward the perfectionists in my life.

BRIAN: It's something that I paid attention to very early in my life in sports. Perfection will never happen, so I worked on the flip side of that and looked at perfection as a state of mind. To know you gave your best with an open heart and your intention was from your heart is all that is needed. That is something that honestly came early in life. In a love relationship, it is more complex, so you have to exercise that discipline even more. Again, if you can look at it from the other side, you're going to be much more in the flow and have more opportunity for love in all areas of your life. There is that opportunity of infinite possibilities if you let go of the idea that your goal is perfection. Getting in the zone in your relationship has nothing to do with perfection and everything to do with making yourself available for unlimited love, care, and appreciation.

Any final words of wisdom you'd like to share?

ARIELLE: If you begin to embrace the Wabi Sabi Love principles, you will have a much happier, stress-free relationship. What it requires is taking a little bit of time to create the intention and attention to live a Wabi Sabi life. The missing piece for many people is emotional maturity. They react to life and their partners without taking a moment to take a deep breath and ask themselves, what would be in the highest and best good in this moment? Oftentimes it would be to do *nothing* as opposed to lashing out. Asking yourself what you could do right now to serve the relationship will ultimately bring more joy and harmony to the partnership.

BRIAN: The Wabi Sabi concept is so important because no one is perfect. Focusing on the differences and imperfections in our partners is divisive. The antidote is love and devotion. The more you open your heart to love and devotion in a relationship, the more you will dissolve those feelings of unhappiness or thoughts that your partner is not perfect enough for you. Devotion is a key ingredient to this. It's not some sort of biblical devotion, but making one's partner a priority and listening to him or her, doing your best to serve your partner and making your relationship come first. When your intention is to create a space of love, wholeness, and healing for each other, you create a container for sacred Wabi Sabi Love.

CONTRIBUTORS

JASON AUSTELL is the morning anchor for a network affiliate in San Diego, California. He is also a lifelong Chargers fan. He can be reached at Jasonaustell@nbc.com.

MOJI AUSTELL is a fitness entrepreneur based in La Jolla, California. She is the co-owner of Pilates United, La Jolla, California's first Pilates studio. (www.Pilatesunited.com)

BARNET BAIN is a metaphysical teacher and lecturer and cohost of radio's *Cutting Edge Consciousness* as well as an award-winning producer and director of films that celebrate the human spirit, including "life after death" Oscar winner *What Dreams May Come* (producer), *The Celestine Prophecy* (producer and screenplay), *The Lost and Found Family* (director), and triple Emmy nominee *Homeless to Harvard* (producer). (www.barnetbain.com)

JOAN BORYSENKO, Ph.D., is a biologist, licensed psychologist, spiritual director, and trainer of spiritual directors. She is author or coauthor of fourteen books and numerous audio and video programs, including the *New York Times* bestseller, *Minding the Body, Mending the Mind,* and her newest book, *Fried: Why You Burn Out and How to Revive.* (www.joanborysenko.com)

LAWRENCE A. COHEN is a New York attorney and a member of the New York State Supreme Court Mediation Panel. Once, fishing in Gloucester, Massachusetts, he lost a 750-pound giant bluefin tuna and has never gotten over it.

SHERRY SUIB COHEN is a *New York Times* bestselling writer of twenty-four books, whose greatest achievement is Lawrence. A. Cohen. (www.sherrysuibcohen.com)

BARBARA "WILLOW" POTTER DRINKWATER, first wife of her fourth and final husband, lives on a horse farm and has been selling real estate since 1981 in the Piedmont of central Virginia. (www.lifeisagodtrip.wordpress.com)

GORDON DVEIRIN coauthored *Your Soul's Compass: What Is Spiritual Guidance?* with his wife, Joan Borysenko.

RAY DUNN is founder of Cutters Run, a waterfowl/guide/hunting service and shop foreman for Motorcycle Madness, New Jersey's largest preowned-motorcycle dealer. He lives with his wife, Jill, in the country with their four-legged children Cutter, Miracle, Sage, and Cali in Independence, New Jersey. (www.cuttersrun.com and www.madmotorcycle.com)

LES GABRIEL is a Haitian-born electrical engineer who has worked on overseas assignments during most of his forty-year-long career. He has lived in Africa, Asia, North and South America, Indonesia, and parts of Europe, including Russia. Les has attended numerous seminars in the field of personal development and credits these teachings for affording him the inspiring life he enjoys. Les is a dedicated family man whose greatest pride are his daughters and grandson.

MIMI GABRIEL is the author of *The Heart to Forgive*, an account of how she overcame the trauma of her husband's infidelity and its devastating effects. Through her counseling battered women, she applied the same tools she had learned while dealing with her own near-shattering experience. Today she claims to be the happiest woman she knows and feels blessed to enjoy a deeper appreciation for her life partner. (www.thehappiestwoman.net)

VIVIAN GLYCK is the founder and executive director of Just Like My Child. A successful author and marketing director, Vivian started Just Like My Child after the birth of her son, Zak, when she realized that all mothers love their children and that all children deserve healthy bodies and a chance to be educated. An author and successful former marketing director for Deepak

Chopra and Glyck Communications, Vivian Glyck currently lives in San Diego with her husband and son, though she is a native New Yorker. She also enjoys Bikram Yoga, bike riding, and spinning. (www.JustLikeMyChild.org)

GAY HENDRICKS has served for more than thirty years as one of the major contributors to the fields of relationship transformation and body-mind therapies. Along with his wife, Dr. Kathlyn Hendricks, Gay is the author of many bestsellers, including *Conscious Loving, At the Speed of Life,* and *Five Wishes.* His latest book, *The Big Leap,* is published by HarperOne. Dr. Hendricks received his Ph.D. in counseling psychology from Stanford in 1974. After a twenty-one-year career as a professor at the University of Colorado, he founded the Hendricks Institute, which offers seminars in North America, Asia, and Europe. (www.hendricks.com)

KATHLYN HENDRICKS is the CEO and director of training for the Hendricks Institute, an international learning organization that teaches the core skills of conscious living through a unique, whole-body approach to Quantum Coaching. She has consulted and taught in the graduate programs of many universities and has an international reputation as a seminar leader for health and business professionals. She is the coauthor of ten books, including *Conscious Loving, The Conscious Heart,* and *Lasting Love.* (www.hendricks.com)

DR. JAY KENT-FERRARO is a recognized expert in optimal-performance coaching and human development, with over two decades of real-life experience as an organizational and clinical psychologist, consultant, certified coach, trainer, author, and speaker (husband and dad to five kids too!). Dr. Jay received postdoctoral training at the prestigious Gestalt Institute of Cleveland, with a specialty in working with small groups and intimate systems, and completed an APA-approved internship with specialties in family psychiatry at the Children's Medical Center. He is a nationally certified psychologist, licensed professional counselor, and certified corporate coach and trainer. With the added degree of MBA, Dr. Jay offers a unique blend of credentials and expertise to his consultancy. Today, his passion is to share the power of his own very personal journey of overcoming infidelity, teaching others how to design lives of their choosing regardless of the circumstances in which people find themselves. (www.surprisedbylove.com)

JULIE KENT-FERRARO is no stranger to the stage or camera. With "quadruple-threat" training in vocal music, dance, acting, and public speaking, Julie has performed in live theater, print, commercials, and motion pictures. She has worked with Coke, Safeway, Otasco, and Sonic, as well as many of the country's top modeling agencies. In 2006, Julie experienced her own nightmares becoming reality when she simultaneously faced a diagnosis of lymphoma and infidelity within her marriage. Her strength, determination, and love for her family prevailed, and she is now proud to call herself a cancer *and* infidelity survivor. Today, Julie is a sought-after speaker by many family, spiritual, and women's organizations. Having been personally trained by Drs. John and Julie Gottman at the Gottman Institute in Seattle, Washington, she also is an affair-recovery coach to couples healing from infidelity. Her most cherished role, however, is being a wife to Jay and a mother to their four beautiful children. (www.surprisedbylove.com)

MICHAEL KOENIGS is a geek, surfer, marketer, video producer, and didgeridoo player, who is best known as the guy who created the Web 2.0 syndication service Traffic Geyser, which distributes over a million videos per week and generates top-ranking web traffic, and leads in minutes by sending video content to over seventy video sites, social bookmarking, social media, blog, and podcasting directories. His clients include Tony Robbins, Paula Abdul, Brian Tracy, and Arielle Ford. Mike's Digital Café studio is located in San Diego, California. (www.mikekoenigs.com)

FRED LUSKIN, Ph.D., is the author of *Forgive for Good* and coauthor of *Stress Free for Good.* (www.learningtoforgive.com)

JAN KRINSLEY LUSKIN always wanted to be a hairdresser when she was a little girl. The dream has now been fulfilled as she manages Fred's hair!

JILL MANGINO is president of Circle 3 Media, a boutique public relations agency specializing in body, mind, and spirit clientele. (www.circle3media.com)

PEGGY MCCOLL is a *New York Times* bestselling author and an internationally recognized speaker, author, mentor, and expert in the area of goal achievement and online marketing. (www.destinies.com)

LAURA MUNSON is the author of the *New York Times* bestselling memoir *This Is Not the Story You Think It Is.* She lives in Montana with her husband and

children. (www.lauramunsonauthor.com and www.lauramunson.wordpress
.com)

SUSAN POHLMAN is the author of *Halfway to Each Other: How a Year in
Italy Brought Our Family Home.* (www.susanpohlman.com and www.susan
pohlman.com/blog)

ROBIN RICE is an internationally published author and mentor to women
leaders. (www.BeWhoYouAre.com and www.UpTribeMedia.com)

ED AND DEB SHAPIRO are the authors of *Be the Change: How Meditation
Can Transform You and the World,* winner of the 2010 Gold Nautilus Book
Award, and the award-winning *Your Body Speaks Your Mind.* They are
featured weekly bloggers for www.oprah.com/spirit and www.huffington
post.com/living.

SANDI STUART is an international licensing and brand management consultant and cofounder of Agency Licensing, LLC.

CLAIRE ZAMMIT, Ph.D., and CRAIG HAMILTON, are cofounders of Evolving
Wisdom, one of the world's leading online learning communities. They are
committed to serving the evolution of consciousness and culture on the
planet by building and nurturing a global transformative learning community that brings visionaries and wisdom teachers together with passionate learners for the purpose of creating deep transformation at all levels.
Claire is the coauthor of the forthcoming book *Feminine Power: Awakening
to the Creative Force of Life,* and cocreator and cohost of the internationally
acclaimed Women on the Edge of Evolution teleseries. Craig is a pioneer
in the emerging field of evolutionary spirituality. In his inspired writings,
talks, and teachings, he calls us to awaken beyond the confines of the separate ego and dedicate our lives to the further evolution of consciousness
itself. (www.evolvingwisdom.com)

ACKNOWLEDGMENTS

Writing this book was quite possibly the biggest challenge of my life. I grappled with levels of fear and insecurity that I haven't reached since taking Public Speaking 101 in college. It really did take a village of loving family and friends to support me through this process.

To my sister, the fabulous Debbie Ford, thank you for allowing me to tap in to your brilliant mind and for giving this book its initial foundation.

To Christine Hohlbaum, my friend and editor, who worked side by side with me (even though you are in Germany), I couldn't have done this without you. Your creative skills, commitment, and sparkling energy are evident on every page.

Big thanks to Robin Rice for compassionately coaching me through my resistance and helping me to embrace my Wabi Sabi destiny.

To the author whisperer, Linda Sivertsen, your magical ability to reorganize words and sentences is always amazing. Thank you for always being there for me.

I have endless admiration and gratitude for Jean Houston for her time and imaginative processes that opened me up to new dimensions and understandings of how to share this information.

For my PR Angel, Jill Mangino, thank you for always caring and for looking for ways to keep spreading the word.

I am exceedingly grateful to the fearless couples who shared their Wabi Sabi stories with me: Arjuna and Chameli Ardagh; Jason and Moji Austell; Joan Borysenko and Gordon Dveirin; Barnet Bain and Sandi Stuart; Diane

Acknowledgments

V. Cirincione, Ph.D., and Jerry Jampolsky; Alanna and Mike Clear; Lawrence Cohen and Sherry Suib Cohen; Barbara "Willow" Potter Drinkwater; Mimi and Les Gabriel; Vivian Glyck and Mike Koenigs; Gay and Kathlyn Hendricks; Dr. Jay and Julie Kent-Ferraro; Fred Luskin and Jan Krinsley Luskin; Jill Mangino and Ray Dunn; Peggy McColl and Denis Beliveau; Laura Munson; Tim and Susan Pohlman; Robin Rice; Ed and Deb Shapiro; Wendy and Frank; and Claire Zammit and Craig Hamilton.

I am blessed to have a wide circle of friends and associates, many of whom contributed in ways big and small, always offering encouragement, ideas, suggestions, and feedback. Many thanks to Amy Ahlers, Carol Allen, Mary Allen, Heide Banks, Reverend Laurie Sue Brockway, Alan Cohen, Randy Collett, Otto and Susie Collins, Rita Curtis, Danielle Dorman, Vic Furman, Rich German, Gail Goodwin, Suzanne Henry, Divina Infusino, Carole Isenberg, Gloria Jones, Peggy La Cerra, Krista Linza and Don Belt, Theresa McGrath, Judy O'Beirn, Nick Ortner, Leize and David Perlmutter, Carla Picardi and Goffredo Chiavelli, Becky Robbins, Kathleen Saver, Faye Schell, Pamela Serure, Lisa Sharkey, Marci Shimoff, Lauren Simon, Elliott Turini, Jai Varadaraj, Kyle and Jean Widner, Dee Winn, and Wyndham Wood.

To my dream team at Harper One, Cynthia DiTiberio, Gideon Weil, Mark Tauber, Suzanne Wickham, Claudia Boutote, Maria Schulman, and Suzanne Quist, thank you for your support and for believing in this book.

For my new family at Evolving Wisdom, thank you for the difference you are making in the world and for inviting me into the circle. I feel honored to be a part of such a talented and dedicated team of evolutionary souls.

Much gratitude to Doc Childre, Deborah Rozman, Howard Martin, and the entire team at the Institute of Heartmath for their pioneering and groundbreaking contributions in the domain of heart intelligence. You have changed and positively impacted my life in ways big and small.

Endless blessings to my mother, Sheila Fuerst, and my mother-in-law, Peggy Hilliard, for the loving and bright light they always shine on us.

Finally, there are no words to describe my deep love and appreciation for the ongoing care, patience, and editing I received from my soulmate and beloved Wabi Sabi husband, Brian Hilliard, who guided me through this process from beginning to end. Thank you for loving me the way that you do. Thank you for always being my safe place to land. I love you.

ABOUT THE AUTHOR

Arielle Ford is a leading personality in the personal growth and contemporary spirituality movement. For the past twenty-five years she has been living, teaching, and promoting consciousness through all forms of media. Her stellar career includes years as a prominent book publicist, author, literary agent, TV lifestyle reporter, television producer, Sirius radio host, publishing consultant, relationship expert, speaker, columnist, and blogger for the *Huffington Post*.

Arielle is a gifted writer and the author of eight books including the international bestseller *The Soulmate Secret: Manifest the Love of Your Life with the Law of Attraction*. She has been called the "Cupid of Consciousness" and the "Fairy Godmother of Love" and believes that with a simple Wabi Sabi shift in perception, couples can discover the beauty and perfection in themselves and their partners, leading to a deeper, more loving, and more fulfilling relationship.

She lives in La Jolla, California, with her husband/soulmate, Brian Hilliard, and their feline friends.

www.arielleford.com